Taekwondo Poomsae 1–8

SANDRO STÜCKLER
Foreword by Stuart Anslow

TAEKWONDO

POOMSAE 1 - 8

MEYER & MEYER SPORT

British Library of Cataloguing in Publication Data
A catalogue record for this book is available from the British Library

Taekwondo Poomsae 1-8
Maidenhead: Meyer & Meyer Sport (UK) Ltd., 2025
ISBN: 978-1-78255-279-6

Original title: *Taekwondo Poomsae 1-8: Die Formen und ihre Bedeutung in der Nahkampfkunst*, © 2022 by Meyer & Meyer Verlag

Aachen, Auckland, Beirut, Cairo, Cape Town, Dubai, Hägendorf, Hong Kong, Indianapolis, Maidenhead, Manila, New Delhi, Singapore, Sydney, Tehran, Vienna
Member of the World Sport Publishers' Association (WSPA), www.w-s-p-a.org

Printed by Versa Press, www.versapress.com
Printed in the United States of America

ISBN: 978-1-78255-279-6
Email: info@m-m-sports.com
www.thesportspublisher.com

Manufacturer under the GSPR
Meyer & Meyer Fachverlag und Buchhandel GmbH
Von-Coels-Str. 390
52080 Aachen
Email: kontakt@m-m-sports.com
www.dersportverlag.de

CONTENTS

Part Two

Preface

Is Taekwondo a realistic martial art?

These days, martial arts are in a state of flux, perhaps more so and faster than ever before. The sharp increase in popularity of Brazilian Jiu Jitsu (which essentially evolved from Japanese Judo) and the subsequent unprecedented evolution of mixed martial arts (MMA), which is a combination of all possible styles to achieve the maximum effectiveness (united under one specific set of rules (Ultimate Fighting Championship, Bellator, etc.)), exposes all martial arts to an unprecedented comparison.

This comparison is completely unique in this global form. Through digital networking, mainly YouTube, it is possible to compete with everyone, or to analyze techniques and strategies and find them useful or, in some cases, completely unsuitable.

This may be a sobering experience for some martial artists and their athletes, masters, etc. For the martial arts as a whole, it is an excellent test. Self-reflection, which was previously left to the individual—"What is my art good for in a serious situation?"—is now even stronger than before as a fundamental question addressed to all martial arts.

Of course, this question has always existed, but the difference today is that the result is on display for everyone to see. Documented thousands of times, commentable, and stored for all (digital) time in the vastness of the internet. So there is little room for ineffective concepts. These exist in abundance, of course. But any possible weaknesses (as well as strengths) of a martial art today are immediately visible to everyone.

So where does Taekwondo stand under these conditions?

Here we have to make a distinction right away: Taekwondo as a competitive sport and Taekwondo as a martial art.

The great success of World Taekwondo (WT) having been accepted into the circle of Olympic disciplines proves to be a double-edged sword here. Because of this success, many schools are completely focused on the competitive aspect of Taekwondo and largely focus their training on the Olympic competition rules.

The focus of these rules, however, is on making fights as fair and spectacular (for the spectator) as possible. This competition has almost nothing to do with self-defense, which is obvious to anyone who has spent even a second thinking about self-defense.

Also, some schools neglect the training of Poomsae forms, as these do not bring any direct added value for success or failure in a (fighting) tournament. This is only natural and sensible, since all resources and time available for training are geared toward achieving the best possible ranking.

Ironically, this development (forgetting of the original intention and the exaggerated form) even affects Poomsae itself in the discipline of form walking. Here, too, the beautiful form (high, vertical kicks upward) is prioritized above the original purpose of the technique.

The second major Taekwondo style (International Taekwon-do Federation (ITF) or "traditional Taekwondo") is in this respect similar. Here, too, the competition rules of the so-called free fight are anything but free. On the contrary, e.g. kicks below the belt are forbidden in light contact. The martial art in the tournament voluntarily deprives itself of its greatest weapon, in order to meet a certain idea of competition.

In general, the discrepancy between martial arts and competitive sports is particularly pronounced in traditional Taekwondo, where Hyungs or Tuls are taught instead of Poomsae.

The Hyungs/Tuls, which have a somewhat more direct lineage to the Chinese styles as well as military close combat and have a wealth of effective techniques (also due to the large number of techniques that directly target pain points and nerve centers), can be considered practically only in isolation and are, in fact, not to be found in competitive sports.

If the true potential of the forms cannot be found in competition, then where can it be found? We will get to the bottom of this riddle in the next chapters. Only in this way can we understand the original power, effectiveness, and elegance of Taekwondo.

Foreword by Stuart Anslow

Making Taekwon-do more than the sum of its parts, and thus more beneficial to both students and instructors, has been a focus of mine for the past 20 years.

I published my first book on realistic application of the forms (Ch'ang On Taekwon-do Hae Sul) in 2005, and others have been published since, expanding the rich variety of realistic applications that any Taekwon-do student can access to improve his or her art and training. While mine and many of the other books study the Ch'ang Hon (ITF) Tuls, there have been few books that focus on realistic applications for the Kukkiwon (WT) Poomsae, with the exception of Simon O'Neill's The Taegeuk Cipher, which was published in 2008. Therefore, it is invaluable to have another author who can provide more material for the broader student base of WT, providing students and instructors with opportunities to improve their art and benefit their training in Poomsae.

To this end, I commend Sabom Stückler for this excellent work and highly recommend it to all students who wish to have a deeper understanding of what their Poomsae really contains and how the knowledge can and will improve their training in Taekwondo.

» Stuart Anslow, is editor of the *Totally Taekwondo* magazine and author of *Ch'ang Hon Taekwon-do Hae Sul* Vol. 1 & 2 as well as many other books on the subject of Taekwondo. He was honored in 2010 by Dr. Choue, President of the World Taekwondo Federation (WT) for his contributions and his "extraordinary achievements in the development of Taekwondo."

1 The true nature of Poomsae... what is visible on the surface and what is beneath it

So we must consider Taekwondo in its originally intended form, independent of competition.

» What did the inventors, the six (or nine) most highly graduated and respected masters of the most important styles (Kwans) of their time, intend to give us?

» What kind of dangers or attacks should we be able to protect ourselves against?

There are some places in the forms that indicate that it is a coded system. For example, sometimes you walk in one direction and perform a block move twice in a row. Then you turn and walk away in another direction.

What happened here? Did our blocking moves render the imaginary attacker unable to fight? You can surely remember one of the sequences—there are several of them.

It would be easy to assume that the developers simply thought nothing of it. Or that they would have judged the potential attacker to be capricious and unimaginative, so that the attacker would keep coming up with the same static attack , finally, for no reason at all, voluntarily refraining from continuing his attack.

Realistically, we can assume the highest possible professional competence as the foundation. The biographies of the designated masters suggest this conclusion. They all had years, even decades, of practical and theoretical training in all known styles of the time and regions.

These include the various styles of Karate, (the ancient ones from Okinawa as well as the reformed ones from mainland Japan), the Kung Fu styles from China, Judo from Japan, and the martial arts of Korea.

As much knowledge and practical experience as possible should be brought in to develop this new martial art. It can be assumed that each master tried to pass on the best of his knowledge, to bring it into Taekwondo.

Considering the Poomsae itself, as well as the context of developing a new martial art, suggests that the following considerations played a role:

The techniques should be as easy and quick to learn as possible, only then can they actually be called on in a stressful situation. Few individual techniques for as many applications as possible should be the goal. Techniques that are difficult to learn and complicated to execute are replaced by simple ones that are just as effective.

Complicated pain point attacks are replaced with simple ones due to the recognized weaknesses (difficult to hit, not equally sensitive to all people, clothing reduces the effect, etc.) introduced in the advanced forms. Multifunctional movements would be best, where the rehearsed (conditioned) reflex is suitable for different scenarios.

Depending on the situation, the application of the technique varies. The ingeniously simple solution is to have a few movements that can be used equally as a defense, attack, or control technique (= leverage) depending on the scenario. As a positive side effect, so to speak, an observer who does not have the knowledge of the specific imagined attack cannot really understand the movements of the practitioner.

Thus, someone who is only watching cannot really learn the martial art because they cannot classify the meaning of the technique. With (martial) arts, it has always been about the element of surprise–to leave outsiders, as far as possible, in ignorance. The knowledge advantage and the surprise effect are and, have always been, the decisive advantage in any kind of fight.

But what happens when the new martial art is so successful that it is no longer passed from one person to another, but from one to hundreds or thousands of students? Quite simply, the explanations and applications fail to materialize, and the pure form survives, meaning that without any guidance, the movements can be (and often are) interpreted incorrectly. Many martial arts have suffered this fate.

Parts of Karate suffer very much the same fate as Taekwondo. The most striking is probably in Tai Chi , the well-known Chinese art of movement, which is practiced daily by thousands of people not only in Chinese parks.

There are clear suggestions that Tai Chi is a forgotten martial art, of throwing and leverage techniques performed against imaginary opponents, and not just the art of movement for a healthy flow of energy and a supple body, as is commonly believed.

The first sentence of this chapter was, "We must consider Taekwondo in its 'pure form'." This meant that the Poomsae (Hyung/Tul) contains all the self-defense-related Taekwondo information. On the other hand, the pure form is exactly what has been copied over the decades, which–copying the form without content–has resulted in the true purpose being partly forgotten.

The Poomsae are not only BLOCK-KICK-PUNCH. The Poomsae contain an exemplary sequence of basic movements that can be used both as liberation, fixation (control), block, (counter) strike, leverage (control or finish), or throwing technique.

After 30 years of Taekwondo practice, I can confirm that the simplicity and ingenuity of this system is captivating. And despite the simple basic structure, there is always something new to discover.

A masterful and intuitive application of the procedures is difficult to achieve without years of training, and yet I believe that Taekwondo, in particular, is a system that both challenges the advanced practitioner and immediately gives the beginner practical tools to better defend themselves.

Of course, this requires the right training in the spirit of the inventor. The motivation behind this book is to discover this sense and, using it as a base, to contribute to effective training with some examples. It may be helpful for you to achieve these goals–and to fathom the true nature of Taekwondo!

"The brilliantly simple solution is to have a few sequences of movements that, depending on the scenario, can be used equally as a defense, attack or control technique (= leverage)."

2 Decoding the movements

2.1 The attack

Based on what we have learned in the previous sections, the first questions we have to ask ourselves are:

- How does the opponent attack?
- How exactly does the attacker threaten us?
- Is the attacker holding us and how?
- Is the attacker about to strike next?
- What is the attacker's distance from us?

In the following illustrations, let's visualize the attacks that we consider most likely in the context of a real-life confrontation:

Fig. 1

Reach to the lapel, one hand loads for a punch.

Fig. 2

Fist punch with the stronger, usually right hand

Fig. 3

Straight fist punch with the jab

Fig. 4

Two-handed grip to the lapel

Fig. 5

Grip with hand to opposite wrist

Fig. 6

Grip with hand to wrist on the same side ("mirror-like")

Clamp/choke, close

Clamp/choke, wide

Of course, there may be many other ways in which an aggressor can approach.

But if we assume that we only need to react when the aggressor really enters a dangerous zone for us, which corresponds to an arm's length, then the number of possibilities is reduced to roughly the number shown in the examples Fig. 1 to Fig. 8.

Self-protection usually means the opposite of "fighting," this should be mentioned here for clarity.

Self-protection is most successful when a fight can be avoided. Every change of the side of the street, ignoring provocation, or possibly running away, is preferable to direct physical confrontation, and is many times safer than the best defense technique!

2.2 Identification of the technique

Let's move on to the second question:

» What phase of the attack are we in, and how do we best deal with it?

If the attacker is already lunging and trying to hit us, for example, it would be inadvisable to directly counter with a strike of our own without paying attention to our cover. We risk a double hit and could take damage ourselves. So we are forced to block the blow first, or at least at the same time, and only then can we counterattack.

The same applies if we are held down. Here we want to free ourselves first to have our hands fully available for possible counterattacks. Possibly a positive freeing technique may be enough to intimidate the opponent and no further action is needed.

A perfect example of this would be "stripping/knocking off" the opponent's hand (with a grip to the wrist) with an Arae Makgi (low block). Correctly executed, that is, struck with the ulna on the radial nerve, this liberation technique is extremely painful, and the probability that the aggressor will lose interest is a given.

Depending on how the situation develops, it may be necessary to follow up, or to control the opponent (e.g., with an armbar), or maybe—with determination to end the situation—possibly follow up with several techniques in succession. For all these situations there are several examples in the Poomsae.

Due to the modular construction, there is always room for maneuver and interpretation by the practitioner. There are techniques that, depending on the situation, can be used once as a block, once as a lever, and can also be used as a blow.

In the case of liberation techniques with Arae Makgi the countermovement with the second hand to the hip is important!

If the grip to the wrist is made with the diagonally opposite side, the block can be used in the standard version from the first Poomsae (Fig. 9).

Fig. 9

Arae Makgi (to the radial nerve) as a liberation technique

If the attack is mirrored, the countermovement goes to the sternum for the optimal effect. Also known as block no. 9 or "bone breaker," as seen in Fig. 10.

In short: The answers to the first and the second question will tell us whether we want to respond with a release, a block, a punch, a leverage technique, or a throw.

Fig. 10

Arae Makgi as a liberation technique, in the case of an equilateral ("mirror-like") attack

2.3 Permanent control

To gain control in a fight, it is necessary to be constantly active or to keep the opponent busy. This is mainly achieved by trying to unbalance and destabilize the opponent with every technique.

On the one hand, this prevents the opponent from successfully using their own techniques against you, and, on the other hand, it will expose weak points in the opponent's position, which can be used for one's own attacks.

Many throwing and leverage techniques are only possible after the opponent has been thrown off balance. The means, the countermovement of the hand, though frequently used here in the Poomsae, is not involved in the action. Again and again, Taekwondo (as well as Karate) is criticized because this countermovement (executed with the hip in Taekwondo) is unrealistic; the hand, which is not in action, should be dedicated to protecting the head instead.

It is correct to assume that only one hand is currently "engaged" with the opponent, but how does it look if we assume that the second hand is also involved in the action? For example, by holding one of the opponent's arms?

The opponent would be simultaneously pulled from their stable stance and twisted to the side. Our own action is thereby strengthened, and the other's is weakened.

In the previous example (Figs. 9 and 10), the Arae Makgi (as a release) doubles the effect of the technique through the countermovement. As one hand pulls toward the body and the other hand pushes away, the velocities of the two hands add up, which results in the (release) strike hitting the opponent's forearm with twice the force.

With a very strong opponent, it is indeed the case that the success of the technique depends on the correct execution of the countermovement.

So we have already learned about two crucial effects of the countermovement:

1. To bring the opponent off balance

2. To increase the effect of our blows

Moreover, the pull to the hip can be read not only as a movement but rather as a concept. A scuffle, a scramble, or a fight is usually not a stringing together of individual movements with a second's pause between each. On the contrary, it is rather an organic whole, where one action leads to the next, and one action flows seamlessly into another.

The countermovement can be understood here as a concept of not letting the opponent "off the hook" once you have got hold of them. To constantly reposition the opponent according to your own intentions and to impose your own fight and, finally, your own will.

Look closely at the pictures in this book with regard to this aspect. In most cases, during a technique, the attacker is pulled by the second hand in some way, making it constantly difficult for the opponent to find a stable position or to realign himself.

In most cases, during a technique, the attacker is pulled by the second hand in some way, to the side or downwards, making it constantly difficult for the attacker to find a stable position or to realign himself.

In this concept is the strongest equivalent in Taekwondo to the philosophical principle of Yin and Yang.

2.4 YIN and YANG

The principle of Yin and Yang is a philosophical concept whose origins go far back into Chinese antiquity.

With the *I Ching (Book of Changes)*, the oldest book in China, which most likely originated between the sixth and the ninth century BC, the consideration that every state must inevitably pass into a certain other (opposite) state, found its most complex form, and sixty-four basic states of life were determined, which subsequently served as a tool for the attempt to predict the future *(I Ching oracle)*.

In its basic form, the meanings given to the Taiji—which is the name of the character and consists of the two components, Yin and Yang—were rather simple and derived from an agricultural context. The original meaning was probably sunny side or shady side of a hill. Events like summer and winter or different sowing and harvest cycles were added.

A simple meaning that was taken from the sign was, for example, "warm clothing in winter and cool clothing in summer" (complementing each other to form a harmonious whole). Irresistibly simple and true in equal measure, a characteristic of Taiji, with all its dual levels of meaning, is still inherent in Taiji today, which is certainly part of the secret of its global success.

Added to this is the memorability of the graphics, as well as the openness to interpretation—everyone may add his favorite pair of antagonists (good–evil, man–woman, heaven–earth, etc.). This is exactly what was and is also done in the martial arts.

And here we come to the point where we look at how the concept of Yin and Yang is reflected in Taekwondo.

In the following, we refer to the Korean version of Yin and Yang. The Korean equivalent of the Taiji sign is called "Taegeuk" and consists of the two parts "Um"' (blue) and "Yang" (red). Taegeuk can be translated as "absolute center" or "highest truth."

The famous Korean Taegeuk ("highest truth"), consisting of the opposing parts Um and Yang.

2.5 Um and Yang in Taekwondo

What does the Taegeuk do now in Taekwondo?

For this purpose, it is necessary to note that Taekwondo is a hard martial art. This refers to how Taekwondo deals with attacks from the opponent. An attacking movement is always countered by a hard defensive movement.

In Taekwondo, therefore, a defensive movement is often technically indistinguishable from an attacking movement! That means that blocks are executed like punches, and blows, in turn, are executed like blocks. In many techniques, all aspects, such as lunging, acceleration, countermovement, and retraction, are identical.

Therefore, in many techniques, when executed without an opponent (as in Poomsae), it is impossible to tell whether the movement is a defense or an attack. This is determined only by the context, that is, by the action of the opponent and the way that we wish to react to it.

So there is no place here for Um (in this case "soft") and Yang ("hard") because the techniques of Taekwondo are, by their nature, always hard. In fact, every block in Taekwondo is, by its very design, aimed at maximum damage. Already the defensive move should cause a maximum of problems to the attacker, possibly already leave him unable to fight.

This is also remarkable in so far as Taekwondo differs here very clearly from other martial arts. A blatant contrast would be, for example, Aikido, which is very soft by nature (or also Hapkido or Wing Chun (constant alternation of giving and taking)).

In Aikido the opponent's attacking energy is used almost exclusively to fight him. The opponent's force is redirected and then turned against him, so he is, in fact, fighting with his own strength. Aikido would therefore be a typically soft martial art.

Thus, in Aikido and Hapkido, it is very easy to identify that the attacker is the Yang part, which the defender opposes with his Um (or Yin) energy. Giving (attack) and receiving (defense) form the entirety of the fight here. (The translation of the Japanese word for block *uke* literally means *to receive*.)

In practice, however, it is not quite that simple, as every Judo, Jiu Jitsu, or Hapkido practitioner knows. In reality, the momentum is constantly changing. One pulls toward, the other pulls away. Both push and shove. And then, at the slightest sign of an imbalance of the opponent, this is exploited and a throw is made.

The practitioner can also form the two poles themself by pushing and pulling, in a short time sequence. Taekwondo goes in a similar direction. The difference is that very often push (punch) and pull are exercised simultaneously. Um and Yang are combined in a single movement!

This may sound a bit abstract, but we will see in the following examples that this is an extremely simple principle, which is constantly used in Poomsae, as well as its possible applications.

The basic layout of the techniques, which always provides a push and a pull component, offers the following advantages:

- » The opponent is prevented from evading
- » The opponent's balance is disrupted
- » The distance and timing of the opponent are disrupted.
- » The effect of the attack is increased, as pressure and traction are combined.

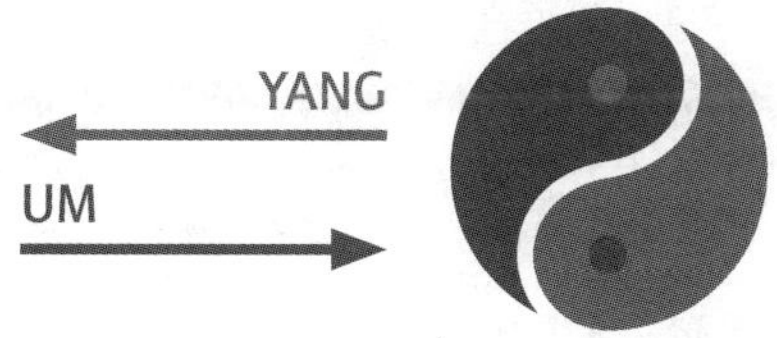

Interpretation of the principle of Um and Yang as a push and pull. The standard execution of the techniques looks exactly like this with the countermovement to the hip—this effect is entirely intentional.

The maximum development of force and effect is achieved by the simultaneous application of the two opposing forces. In the Poomsae, Yin and Yang usually express themselves as pressure and (opposing) pulling force! In the coming chapters, notice how often we will encounter this principle!

2.6 Orientation

- The movements of the Poomsae are numbered consecutively according to the known sequence
- Orientation of the practitioner and the viewer
- The observer always stands opposite the Poomsae practitioner. At the end of the Poomsae, at least when the practitioner walks straight backward in the form (i.e., away from the viewer), they walk diagonally backward in the photo for better visibility.
- When the practitioner approaches the viewer, they usually walk straight forward. If the application is shown in pairs, the direction changes to a slight diagonal if necessary for visibility of the technique. This is also the case if the Poomsae is performed alone. This is to ensure the best possible view for the viewer.

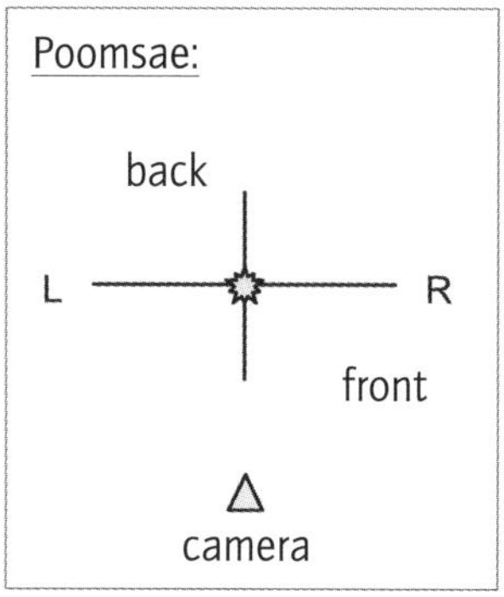

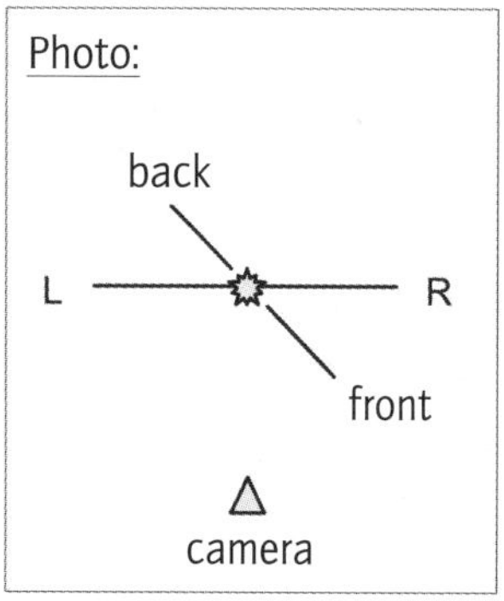

Part One

3 The Poomsae Forms 1–4

3.1 Taegeuk Il-Jang

1

2

3

4

Fig. 11

Fig. 12

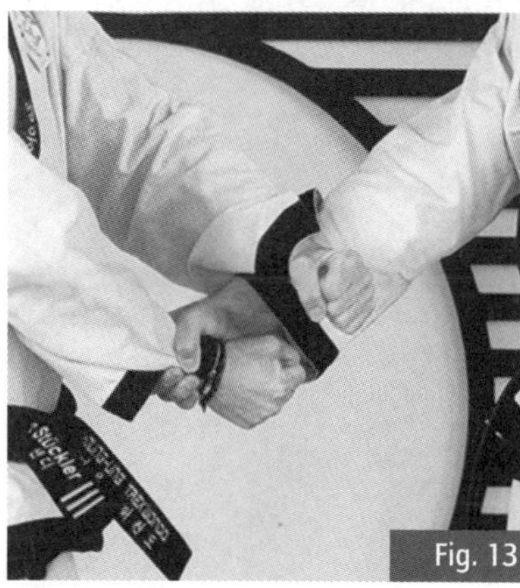
Fig. 13

Arae Makgi (Hadan Makgi) as a liberation technique

The most important facts about "Poomsae 1" at a glance:

Introduction of the simplest release technique against a grip to the wrist (Arae Makgi, or low block). Introduction of simple middle defense and application as an elbow lever (Momtong Palmok An-Makgi, or middle block). Introduction of the high block or Olgul-Makgi as a strike to the opponent's neck or chin. Introduction of the basic sequence of release–counterattack and finishing technique. Simple throwing techniques with turns.

Fig. 11

Fig. 12

The basis here is a grip of the aggressor to the wrist on the opposite side (i.e., the attacker's right hand to the defender's right wrist).

The simultaneous and decisive execution of the countermovement is of particular importance for the effective execution of the release by knocking off (or stripping) the opponent's hand.

The subsequent fist strike shows a possible conclusion to the defense.

Note: If attacked with the same side of the body ("mirror-like"), the defense is also possible, but in this case, the execution with the countermovement in the direction of the sternum is more advisable. (see technique "bone crusher" block, Fig. 10).

5.1

Fig. 14

5.2

Fig. 15

The low block forward, especially in combination with a turn, can be seen as a throwing technique over the defender's thigh. Due to the low center of gravity, the defender is at an advantage and can destabilize the attacker. After the opponent has been brought down, the kick is finished with a fist strike. This technique would be applicable after a choke from the side or a "headlock." Please note that the primary use of this move is as a release or block. Keep in mind, however, that in different scenarios, different ways of using the movement may be possible.

6

Fig. 16

A Momtong Makgi as a hammer fist strike

One variation here is to use the center block as a hammer fist attack to the opponent's lower jaw. The opponent is brought off balance with the countermove. The fist strike completes the action.

7

Fig. 17

Principle of push and pull

8

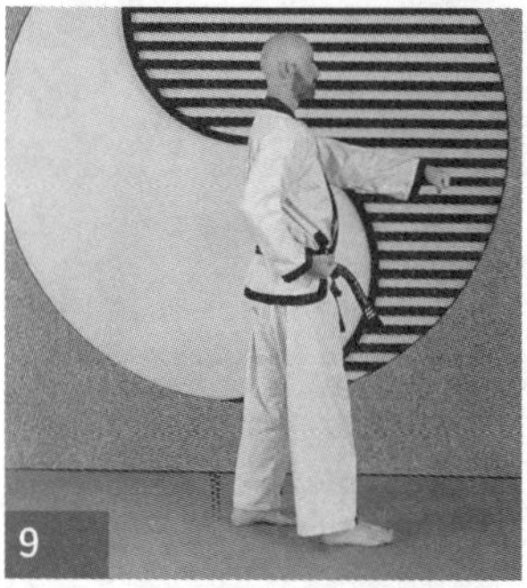

9

10.1

10.2

Fig. 18

Fig. 19

Variation 2 shows the block as an arm lock, which is then abandoned to finish with a fist strike. By using the lever as an opening, the attacker is drawn into the subsequent punch.

Note the second hand pulling on the elbow of the opponent

Kicks are used in self-protection usually below waist level

High block: The opponent holds on to the lapel. The high block is executed as a blow with the forearm (ulna) to the opponent's neck or chin. The opponent is thereby pushed backward. At the same time, the technique is a distraction and initiates the subsequent kick, which is thus more difficult to block. Note the deflection pattern: Up–Down!

To distract the opponent and increase the probability of hitting the target, a successive attack at different heights is effective!

12.2

13

14.1

14.2

Fig. 22

Fist thrust to the neck. The countermovement controls the attacker.

Fig. 23

The high block frees you from a grip to the shoulder

In Fig. 21, the fist strike is executed to the neck. The second hand plays an important role, it controls the opponent's hand and prevents him from evading the blow.

In Fig. 23 we assume that the attacker is holding the defender by the shoulder. The high block here again is a release technique, before finishing with a fist strike again.

15

Fig. 24

Arae Makgi as a throwing technique

16

Fig. 25

Also in this sequence (Fig. 24), the turn can also be used as a throwing motion over the thigh of the defender. The opponent is brought off balance with the forearm. After he tries to get back up, the move is finished with a fist strike (Fig. 25).

A close look at the movements and concepts of the first Poomsae proves to be very useful, since the understanding of the movements of the first form provides an excellent basis for deciphering and understanding the advanced forms!

1

Fig. 26

2

Fig. 27

3

4

Fig. 28

3.2 Taegeuk I-Jang

The most important facts about "Poomsae 2" at a glance:

» Variation of techniques from Poomsae 1. Fist punch with low body center of gravity. Fist punch to the head

» New: Execution of the same movement pattern twice in a row as block–punch or lever.

» New: Quick sequence of several attacks in succession–determined action and striving for a quick conclusion

Fig. 26

Fig. 27

The first movement is again understood as a release from a grip to the wrist. The subsequent fist strike to the body is executed by the defender in a deep stepping position (Apgubi Seogi). This increases the range of the following blow and gives it more power forward. At the same time, the defender remains in a strong forward movement, which makes it difficult for the opponent to keep their balance or to counterstrike.

Momtong-An-Makgi elbow lever from the other direction

We have already learned the center block as a punching technique and as an arm lever in Poomsae 1. Here we assume an arm lever with the first Momtong Makgi (induced by the rotation).

The second center block is probably a hammer fist (to the lower jaw) and a finishing technique, as the direction of movement in the Poomsae is then changed.

7

8.1

8.2

Fig. 32

The counter movement locks the opponent's hand (!)

Fig. 33

This time the low block is used to pull (and control) the opponent. The kick can be to the abdomen, as a knee strike or a sweeping technique to destabilize the opponent. Here a knee kick to the solar plexus is shown.

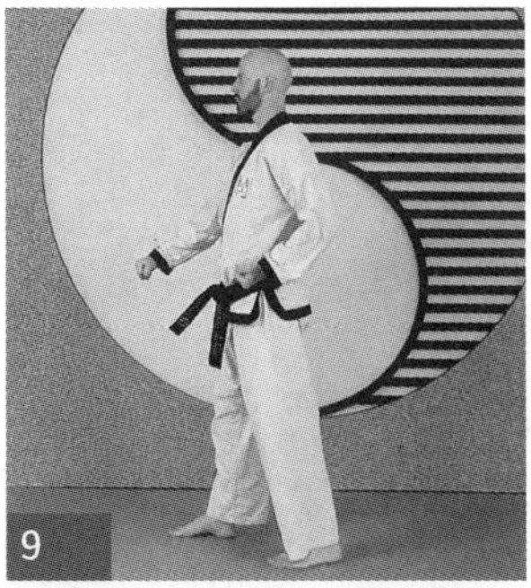

9

10.1

10.2

Fig. 34

Fig. 35

In example number two, controlling the opponent's arm is followed by a front kick and a punch to the head

11

12

Fig. 36

Also have a look at Fig. 20, to see the technique from the side!

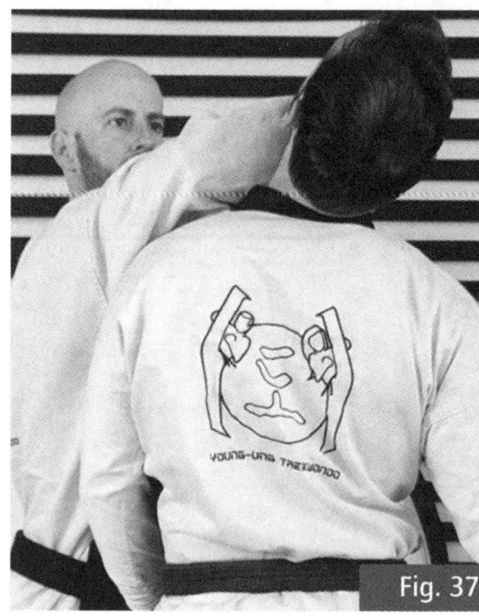

Fig. 37

The high blocks here are blows with the forearm to the lower jaw of the attacker to free oneself from a stranglehold at a close distance.

Caution: The hand performing the countermovement pulls the attacker's arm downwards, and thus increases the effect of the release blow. The technique is executed twice, including the release and the counterattack.

13

Fig. 38

14

Fig. 39

Momtong-An-Makgi as hammer fist knockout punch

In sequences 13 and 14, two things are crucial:

The first Momtong An-Makgi comes from a twisting movement, which favors its applicability as an arm lever and makes it seem likely. As shown in fig. 38.

Furthermore, the second Momtong An-Makgi (center block) ends the action for the current movement axis. Here we have either routed or opponent with our terrifying block, or, more likely, the movement is a hammer fist strike to the lower jaw. After the knock-out punch, no further resistance would be expected here, and movement can be in a new direction.

15

Fig. 40

16.1

Fig. 41

16.2

17.1

Fig. 42

17.2

Fig. 43

Rapid sequence of a fist punch (here to the larynx) . . .

18.1

Fig. 44

. . Ap-Chagi (Front Kick) into the genitals . . .

18.2

Fig. 45

. . . and another fist punch to the neck of the opponent

Note that the opponent is always held with the second hand. This prevents him from moving into the desired position. At the same time, he cannot dodge.

The final passage of the second Poomsae consists of techniques that have already been introduced. The repeated execution of the combination at the end of the form is remarkable. Here a forceful approach to the finish is clear. The opponent is to be overrun, or it is to be granted that there is no more opportunity for a new attack attempt. The decisive approach at the end–after several previous control or defense attempts–appears here for the first time as a concept at the end of the second Poomsae.

3.3 Taegeuk Sam-Jang

1

2.1

2.2

2.3

Fig. 46

Fig. 47

Fig. 48

The most important things about "Poomsae 3" at a glance:

» Many of the movements that we learned in the first and second Poomsae, will be repeated in the third Poomsae. Therefore, we will not explain every single movement again, but let the pictures do the talking.

» Please try to develop a feeling for the movements. The most important points are briefly summarized in the descriptions.

» Although a new movement, namely the knife hand block (Han Sonnal Bakkat Makki) is added, the principles remain the same. Further examples of liberations with subsequent levers and strikes are demonstrated at the end.

Fig. 46

The attacker holds the defender with his right hand on the lapel (see Attacks: Fig. 1). In defense, the left hand strikes with the Arae Makgi (low block) to the crook of the elbow to pull the opponent. The defender's right hand takes control of the attacker's arm for control.

A knee kick to the solar plexus shows here a variation to the ApChagi, the forward kick shown in the Poomsae. Immediately after the leg is set down (or at the same time), a fist thrust follows on the same side, again led into the stomach area.

Fig. 47

Fig. 48

We assume a grip to the lapel as an attack. The opponent is controlled and held. The blow to the crook of the elbow pulls him toward us. Attention to blows with the right hand!

Fig. 49

The second technique is a kick with the left foot to the inner thigh. This destabilizes the opponent.

Fig. 50

Fig. 51

Here it should be noted that the kick to the right thigh of the aggressor naturally prevents him from striking with the right hand. The punch is still possible in principle, but is at least made more difficult by the kick, because the defender with the leg kick here tends to have a range advantage over the attacker's fist attack.

A punch with the left fist in the solar plexus follows. In the Poomsae, another fist punch with the other hand follows afterwards.

3

Fig. 49

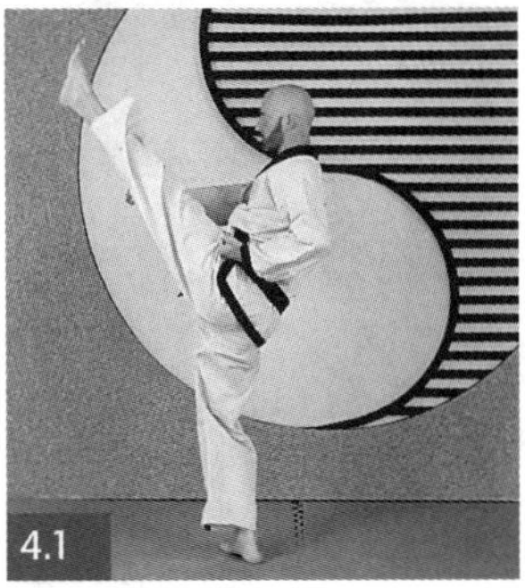
4.1

Fig. 50

4.2

Fig. 51

4.3

5

Fig. 52

6

Fig. 53

7

Fig. 54

8

Fig. 55

The hand that executes the block here, then grips the arm...

Fig. 56

. . . and pulls the opponent into the blow!

Fig. 57

The same arm is furtherly worked with an elbow lever

13

Fig. 58

Liberation with Arae Makgi against a grip to the wrist . . .

14.1

Fig. 59

Ap-Chagi with the right leg, the hand on the left grabs the opponent . . .

14.2

14.3

Fig. 60

. . . and pulls him into the follow-up stroke movement

15

Fig. 61

16.1

Fig. 62

16.2

16.3

Fig. 63

The counter movement to the hip prevents evasion

17.1

Fig. 64

17.2

Fig. 65

18.1

18.2

Fig. 66

Arae Makgi is shown here as a shoulder or elbow lever

19.1

Fig. 67

The kick to the thigh brings the opponent off balance . . .

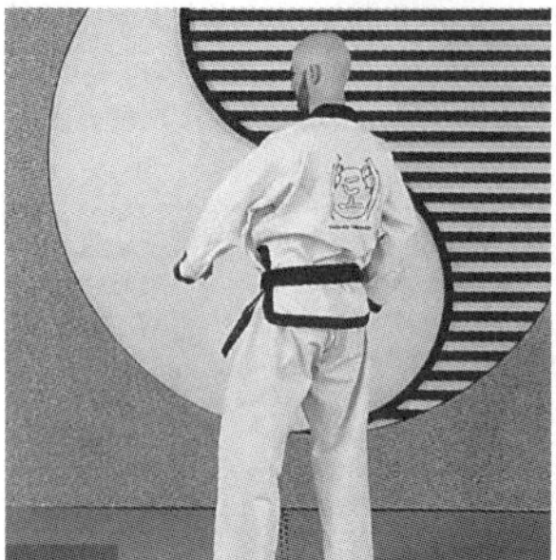
19.2

Fig. 68

Arae Makgi as pressing down of the opponent (against the neck) . .

19.3

Fig. 69

. . . the sequence is finished with a fist punch

With the kick off balance, the opponent is then pressed down with the low block (Arae Makgi).

20.1

Fig. 70

The Ap-Chagi kicks here to the inner thigh.

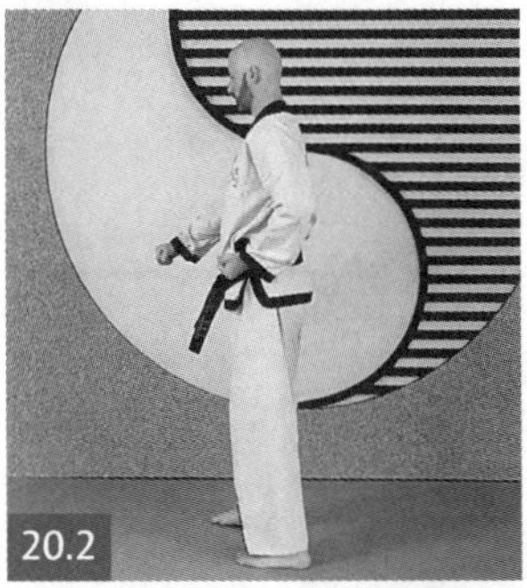
20.2

Fig. 71

The arae-makgi pulls a little further out here to achieve a shoulder lever

20.3

Fig. 72

The right hand keeps its position and the left hand finishes

Let's take a closer look at the last passage, i.e. the movements that go backward at the end of the form. Here we repeat the scheme we learned at the end of Poomsae 2. The opponent is covered with a sequence of fast actions and there is no more escape.

The scheme:

Block – Punch, Block – Punch, Kick – Block – Punch, Kick – Block – Punch

can and should be modified here according to the situation. It is important to always stay in contact with the aggressor and not to give him a chance to readjust himself.

He is constantly being pulled and thrown off balance.

We look at the last three movements again in detail:

Fig. 70

We control the hand from the previous technique and apply an ApChagi to the inner thigh to disrupt the attacker's balance.

Fig. 71

The hand is still controlled. Now an elbow-shoulder lever (with the Arae Makgi low block movement) is followed up with the right hand to further restrict the opponent's freedom of movement.

The lever goes into a pulling motion and opens the side for the final fist punch. Due to the preceding movements, the opponent is hardly able to use his second hand for defense. He also sees the punch coming through the side position (if at all) only very late.

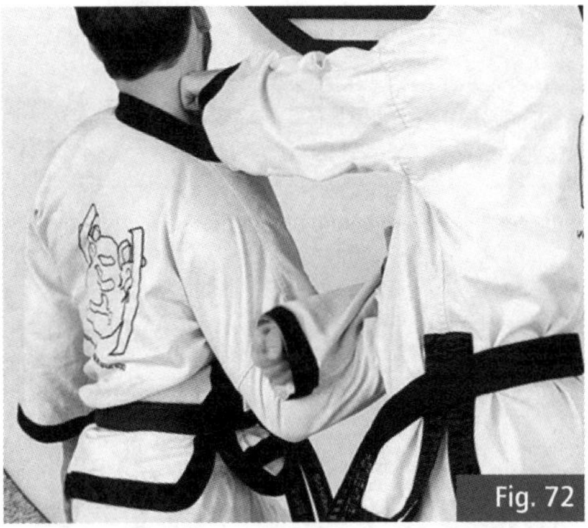

Fig. 72

3.4 Taegeuk Sa-Jang

Sonal-Bakkat-Makgi (SudoTaebi-Makgi) as control technique

Sonal-Bakkat-Makgi (SudoTaebi-Makgi) as block technique

Sonal-Bakkat-Makgi (SudoTaebi-Makgi) as attack technique

The most important facts about "Poomsae 4" at a glance:

» The fourth Poomsae begins with two new movements, namely the Sonal-BakkatMakgi (open hand block), and the Pyeonsonkeut-Jireugi (finger thrust).

» Both movements are particularly interesting and worth a closer look.

» The first movement, the Sonal-Bakkat-Makgi, is one of the central multifunctional defensive movements of Taekwondo. By the kind of its execution it is suitable for the defense of all straight and curved fist strikes. So here we are dealing with the attacks from Figs. 1, 2, and 3, whereby it does not matter whether the fist strike is executed as a straight or a hooked fist punch.

» The ideal execution of the technique would be to interrupt the opponent already in the initial phase of the movement. To do this, the forearm or the edge of the hand strikes the elbow bend of the aggressor or pushes the attack arm back. The earlier the intervention happens, the less force the attack can develop.

» The technique can also be used completely preventively, i.e. as a control technique (see Fig. 73). Here, the blocking arm blocks the elbow bend of the attacker BEFORE the strike. And prevents him in advance from executing the strike. The second hand is used to control the arm holding the lapel (cf. fig. 75).

» Exactly the same technique can still be used as an attacking technique. And this is exactly what the fourth Poomsae demonstrates, at the end of the forward movement no. 10. The fact that the movement is presented before the change of direction indicates that. It would not be logical to turn away from the opponent after a blocking move. After a blow to the neck with the edge of the hand, however, it is possible that the attacker is now incapacitated and we can turn to new targets!

Fig. 76

Pyeonsonkeut-Jirugi (Finger Thrust) as a take down

Fig. 77

The right leg prevents an evasion of the opponent

So here we have again one movement pattern and at least three applications:

1. control technique
2. block technique and
3. strike-attack technique.

We have already discussed this (multipurpose) structure of Poomsae in chapter 1.

Equally interesting is the second technique, the fingertip thrust (PyeonsonkeutJireugi or Kwansu-Tulki).

The most common explanation for this move is that it involves stabbing the solar plexus area with the outstretched fingertips, which is supposed to shock the opponent.

There are always demonstrations to see, where, mostly masters, smash boards with their fingertips. Those who are trained and hardened in such a way may be able to execute the technique in an effective manner. For most normal mortals, however, this application is simply not practicable.

I would also not advise advanced students to use this technique in a stressful situation. In addition to the risk of injury to the defender himself, there are other factors that make question a successful execution.

For example, if the sternum is hit instead of the solar plexus, the technique is basically ineffective. If the aggressor is well trained and has strong abdominal muscles, the area for an effective hit is very small. Clothing such as jackets and the like further reduce the effect additionally.

Last but not least, I could add that in hundreds of MMA and similar fights under rules without closed gloves, this technique has NEVER been successfully applied.

If the blow is led in the direction of the neck, the effectiveness may increase a little, but here again there is the well-known pain-point problem (it is difficult to hit exactly), and the execution in the Poomsae is clearly at the level of the solar plexus.

This also leads us directly to another, far less known, but much more likely variant of the technique.

Pyeonsonkeut-Jireugi as a takedown of the opponent:

Here the step is placed behind the leg of the attacker. At the same time he is prevented from backing away by grasping his back in the area of the lumbar spine.

The thrusting movement is executed with strong pressure of the forearm in the direction of the sternum and then downwards. The attacker is jerkily knocked to the ground.

Attention: The front leg of the defender stands at the back of the attacker and locks the attacker's leg (Fig. 79).

1

Fig. 78

The block with the left forearm is followed by a . . .

2

Fig. 79

. . . pressure/push (= takedown) with the right forearm.

3

4

Fig. 80

5

Fig. 81

Liberation from an embrace with blow to the neck

6.1

Fig. 82

When the opponent is very close the kick becomes a knee strike

6.2

7

Fig. 83

A sidekick goes in self-protection best to the knee . . .

The fifth technique is also new. The Jebipum-Sonal-Mok-Chigi (also Jebipum An-Chigi) is a combination of a high block (Olgul-Makgi or Sangdan-Makki) and a hand edge strike to the neck (Sonal-Mok-Chigi or Sudo-Mok-Taerigi).

This technique is very suitable to get out of a clinch (clamps from the front). It involves pushing one of the opponent's hands away with the high blocking movement upwards. This serves at the same time as a distraction and preparation for the following blow to the neck with the knife hand.

The decisive factor is the jerky lateral twisting of the shoulders (the characteristic of the Jebipum movement (= swallow flight)). The techniques can be executed either in quick succession or simultaneously. For maximum effect, the hand edge strike should be executed at the carotid artery at about the level of the larynx.

Caution is advised when practicing, the special nerve point1[1] at this point can cause the partner to faint. This exercise is therefore recommended without or with only light contact.

1 The glomus caroticum controls blood pressure in the body and reports to the brain. If the blood pressure is apparently too high (due to the blow), abdominal arteries, for example, are dilated and there may be a sudden drop in blood pressure, leading to fainting may occur (cf. Maluschka, 2009).

8.1

Fig. 84

. . . more precisely to the inside of the knee.

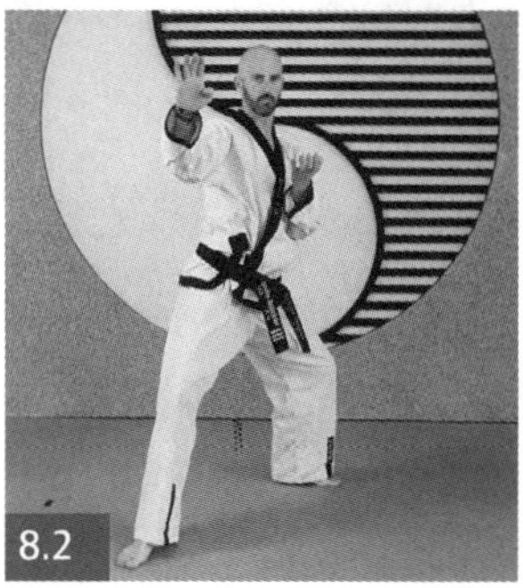
8.2

Fig. 85

A hand edge block, here executed as a blow to the neck.

Sonal-bakkat-mok-chigi as a blow with the forearm or the edge of the hand to a nerve point on the carotid artery.

Alternative interpretation of the technique No. 10: Here, instead of the knife hand an elbow strike to the temple of the opponent is used as a finishing technique.

Fig. 86

Alternatively, the elbow strike to the side/back of the skull could be used.

9

Fig. 87

10.1

Fig. 88

10.2

Fig. 89

A Judo twist throw, as an option

The sequence shows a throwing technique by twisting the opponent. As an introduction the attacker's leg is attacked. As soon as he shifts his weight to the other leg, the throwing-twisting movement is executed.

11

Fig. 90

The shoulders are twisted sideways, the grip loosened . . .

12.1

Fig. 91

. . . the kick against the leg destabilizes the opponent . . .

12.2

Fig. 92

. . . the left hand pulls down and throws the opponent.

13

Fig. 93

14.1

Fig. 94

14.2

Fig. 95

Note how the left hand grasps the opponent after the first technique (no. 13) and then does not let go until the sequence is finished (Fig. 93-95)! The finishing move is a back fist strike to the temple, ear or lower jaw.

15.1

Fig. 96

15.2

Fig. 97

16.1

Fig. 98

16.2

17.1

Fig. 99

17.2

Fig. 100

17.3

Fig. 101

In Fig. 96 and Fig. 97 you can see very nicely, how the defensive movement of the defender's left hand smoothly transitions into the control position, finally pulling the attacker by the sleeve.

18.1

Fig. 102

18.2

Fig. 103

18.3

In Figs. 102 and 103 it is shown how the hand that executed the block remains in its position for control until the subsequent strike is executed. This variation of the technique appears in the older forms (cf. Hyeong 16). We show it here as an alternative to the standard variant. Since the defender is already on the back (blind side) of the opponent in Fig. 102, this version is used to take advantage of the position and to block the arm of the attacker.

3.5 Geographical identification: Which martial arts have shaped Taekwondo?

The influences on the art of Taekwondo

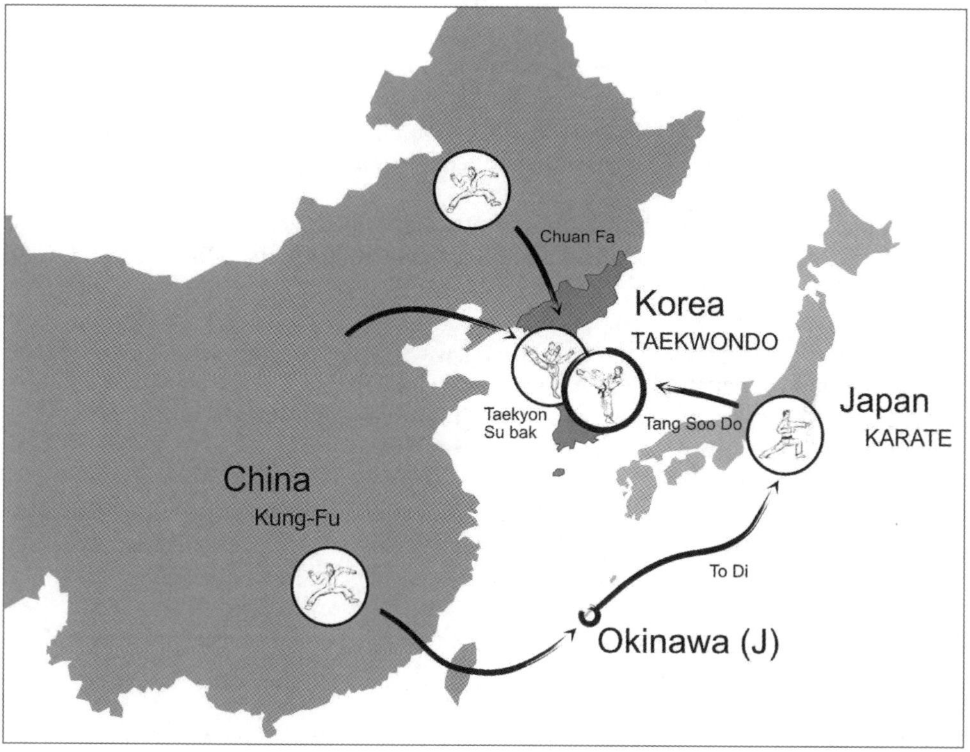

The interrelationships among the martial arts form a complex web. Strongly simplified the following can be crystallized:

Chinese Kung Fu came to Korea in two ways, the first way was directly across the border in the north and the second via a detour from Okinawa to the main Japanese island. And then later through the training and or captivity of many Koreans in Japan, (as Karate) back to Korea.

Here, however, Kung Fu had already gone through several processes of transformation, so that the various styles of Japanese Karate emerged from it, which we want to see as the second component. So Component 1 would be Kung Fu, Component two would be Karate.

Of course, the Karate styles also had various local and international influences, which we do not want to treat here in all their complexity. The Karate that was imported back to Korea was mainly called Tang Soo Do (the Chinese hand).

The third component of Taekwondo are the original styles of Korea like the Taekkyon or Su Bak as well as the Kwon Bop. In the case of Taekkyon and Su Bak sources point out that the terms are used synonymously, i.e. that they are essentially the same or at least a similar martial art.

Both are attributed to the Silla dynasty (Three Kingdoms period, 1st-7th centuries n. Chr.) to assign. Whereas the Kwon Bop is assigned to the Gogeureo dynasty. At least one of the five founding styles (later nine) of modern Taekwondo (WT) a strong connection to the Japanese Judo is provable.

Here the founder of the YUN-MOO style (style = Kwan) took over the former Judo Dojang (Dojang = school/studio) of his master and turned it into a Tang Soo Do school.

Modern Taekwondo can therefore be confidently understood as an amalgam of the great Asian styles KungFu, Karate, Judo and the Korean martial arts such as Taekkyon and Kwon Bop.

As a "best of" the martial arts of the time, it was always subject to processes of transformation and simplification in particular, which is well recognizable in the case of the Poomsae. Much of what was complicated, unnecessary or difficult to learn, was eliminated and only the most important and essential aspects should be preserved.

In architecture, there is the process of "classical modernism" (from circa 1920). By this is meant that one got rid of all frills of the antique building arts and designed and built only following the function, one calls this "form follows function."

This lack of frills and the "simple elegance" is clearly visible in the Poomsae and is one of the trademarks of modern Taekwondo.

This is especially noticeable in Poomsae 1-4. The second part is now dedicated to the somewhat more complex, but still elegant sequences of Poomsae 5-8.

TANG SOO DO: Korean form of Karate. Literally way of the Chinese hand. (Tang = China, Soo = hand, Do = way).
As "Korean Karate" Tang Soo Do is also a mixture of Karate, Chuan Fa (Kung-Fu) and old Korean styles.

Kong Soo Do: Korean form of Karate. Literally the way of the empty hand.
Kong Soo Do and Tang Soo Do both refer to Korean Karate.

KWON BOP (or Gweon Beop): Multiple meanings, both synonymous with **TANG SOO DO**. As well as one of the traditional martial arts of Korea. The roots of the words go back more to the unarmed martial arts of Gogeureo (Time of the Three Kingdoms).

Su Bak (later Soo Bakh Do): Multiple meanings, both synonymous with TANG SOO DO, as well as one of the traditional martial arts of Korea. The roots of the words go back to the unarmed martial arts of Silla (time of the three kingdoms).

TAEKKYON: A traditional Korean martial art, which includes a large number of kicks, punches, and throws. High kicks, jumps, and athletic kicking techniques are the specialty.

(Subak or Soo Bahk Do are synonyms of Taekkyon, so they are the same martial art.)

Hwarang: The legendary warriors of the (unified) Silla dynasty (645-935 AD), similar to the Japanese samurai, but the Hwarang existed from the 7th century AD, around 500 years before the samurai. The Hwarang possessed a code of virtues, diverse training in the martial arts, and their courage and invincibility were proverbial.

https://en.wikipedia.org/wiki/Hwang_Kee

https://de.wikipedia.org/wiki/Taekgyeonhttps://de.wikipedia.org/wiki/Hwang_Ki

https://de.wikipedia.org/wiki/Taekgyeon

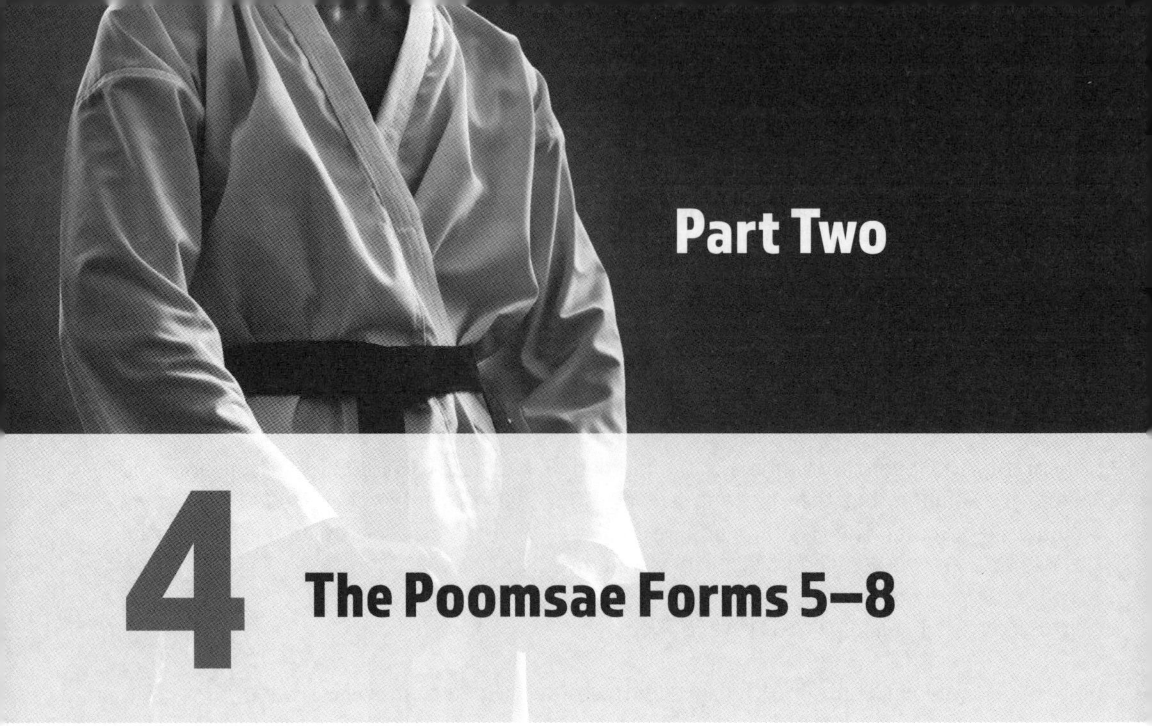

Part Two

4 The Poomsae Forms 5–8

4.1 Taegeuk Oh-Jang

1

Fig. 104

The hammer fist punch to the abdomen as a distraction technique. The blue line shows the possible head movement for liberation

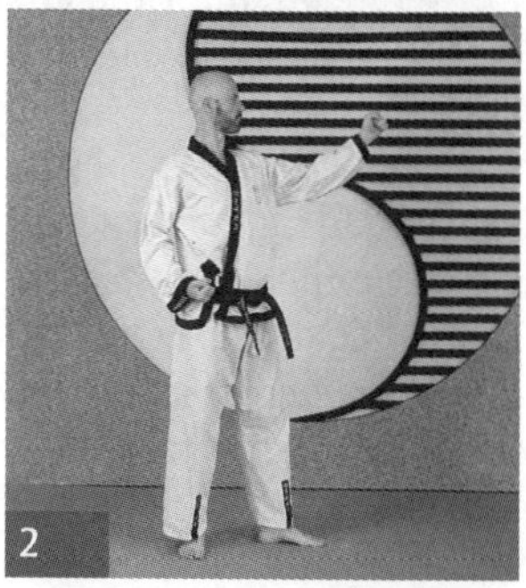
2

3

Fig. 105

The low block pulls the opponent (after a grip to the lapel)

4

Fig. 106

The following hammer fist blow aims at the tip of the nose

The most important things about "Poomsae 5" at a glance:

» The fifth Poomsae shows us some new moves, among them are the hammer fist strike (Me-Jumok-Chigi) and an elbow strike to the inside (Palkup-An-Chigi). There will be a second type of elbow strike, namely the type where the opponent is held back at the back or the neck while the thrust is being performed. The fact that the attacker can be held behind the head at all makes it clear that (even after the Yop-Chagi, which is actually a medium distance technique) it is still a close combat situation.

» The opening sequence of the form is also interesting. The low block here can be interpreted as a distraction technique to the opponent's thigh or abdomen, which opens up the possibility for the subsequent strike in the first place. The hammer fist strike can also be interpreted as a liberation technique. The movement of the head (after the low block) is shown in Fig.104.

» Another hint that we want to stay in hand-to-hand combat until the end of the confrontation also forms the conclusion of the Poomsae. The jumping (dung-jumok-chigi) ends the form. The cross stance is used to shorten the distance to the opponent in a flash. The rotating movement of the hips makes it easier for us to defend against any attacks from the opponent that may occur at the same time. Furthermore, the end position (hip to hip, the center of gravity of the opponent is very close to our body), on our part, gives us a possibility to put a throwing technique to the end. This throwing technique is not shown in the fifth Poomsae specifically, but there are still some throws in the black belt forms and the traditional Hyungs. The fifth Poomsae, through the footwork, clearly lays the foundation for a throw.

5.1

Fig. 107

The center block positions us on the blind side of the opponent

5.2

Fig. 108

The second center block is interpreted as an arm lever . . .

6.1

Fig. 109

. . . directly followed by a (Ap-Chagi) kick to the genitals

6.2

Fig. 110

The kick is immediately followed by a backfist strike to the head

6.3

Fig. 111

Hammer fist again, note the second hand (control)

7.1

Fig. 112

The Ap-Chagi – here used as a knee strike again

7.2

Fig. 113

Alternative execution of the backfist strike, as . . .

7.3

Fig. 114

8

Fig. 115

. . . a downward elbow strike

9

Fig. 116

10

Fig. 117

11

12

Fig. 118

13.1

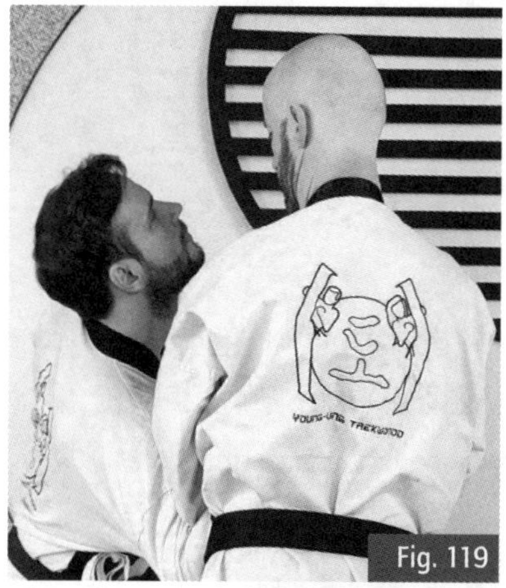

Fig. 119

13.2

Fig. 120

Caution: Elbow techniques such as those in Fig. 117 and Fig. 118 only work in very close range. This makes the pulling and controlling movement of the second hand even more important. Not only does this increase the effect of the technique, it also prevents the opponent from dodging. An alternative execution of the technique, which also increases the likelihood of success is to hold the opponent by the scruff of the neck, as we will see next in Fig. 126!

14.1

14.2

14.3

Fig. 121

Fig. 122

The "low block" as a shoulder lock

Fig. 123

The "middle block" as a hammer fist to the back of the head

15

Fig. 124

The high block releases the grip to the shoulder . . .

16.1

Fig. 125

. . . Side kick (Yeop-Chagi) and hammer fist follow up . . .

16.2

Fig. 126

. . . the elbow strike finishes off, the second hand holds the neck!

17

Fig. 127

18.1

Fig. 128

18.2

Fig. 129

19.1

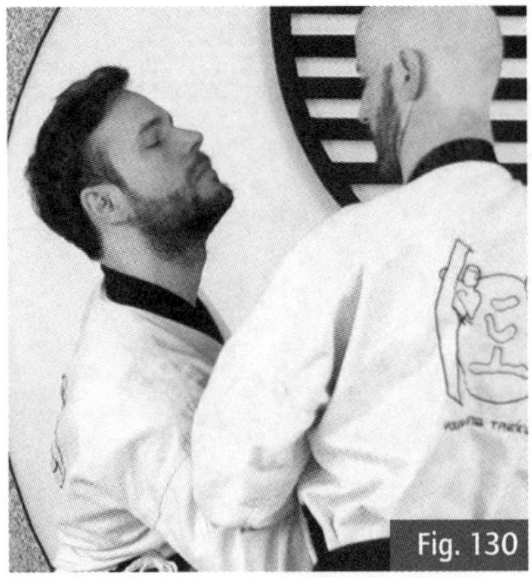

Fig. 130

The attacker is being pulled toward us...

19.2

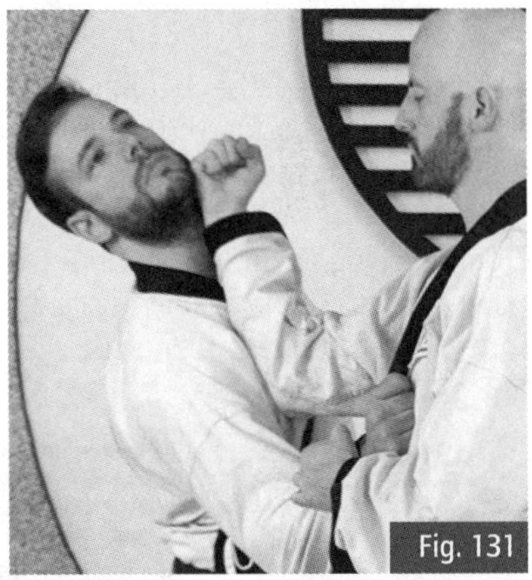

Fig. 131

. . . the hammer fist knockout blow follows from a close range

20.1

Fig. 132

In close combat, the Ap-Chagi can become a knee strike!

The low block fixes the opponent's arm (Fig. 130). The middle block is used as a hammer fist to the lower jaw (Fig. 131). The Ap-Chagi kick is shown here as a possible knee strike (Fig. 132)

20.2

Fig. 133

The end of the fifth Poomsae is particularly interesting due to the footwork shown.

As mentioned at the beginning of the chapter, the jumped-in cross stance offers the opportunity to bridge the distance to the opponent in a flash. A technique is immediately applied here, namely the back fist strike (Deung-Jumeok-ApChigi) (Fig. 133).

From here you could ideally finish with a throwing technique. The throw is not shown in the Poomsae, but the possibility is clearly opened up. In advanced Poomsae (and Hyungs) more throwing techniques are indicated. The execution of the possible hip throw can be seen here in Fig. 134 and 135.

Fig. 134

The triceps lever forces the opponent on his toes . . .

Fig. 135

. . . the upper body needs to be pulled downwards and twisted simultaneously.

4.2 Taegeuk Yuk-Jang

1

Fig. 136

The low block controls the position of the opponent . . .

2.1

Fig. 137

. . . as a follow-up technique the Ap-Chagi (Front Kick) is used.

2.2

Fig. 138

The forearm block with the fist turned forward (Fig. 138).

Palmok-Momtong Bakkat Makgi – as a forearm punch. Turning the fist forward makes particularly sense in this case, as the ulna is used for striking.

The most important facts about "Poomsae 6" at a glance:

» In the sixth Poomsae we again find some possibilities to deal with clinching. New and worth emphasizing here is the possibility of the forearm strike (with the ulna) to the neck or lower jaw. The forearm strike with the outer edge of the arm is a powerful and effective tool. The attack is indicated here by the fact that it is used to finish the (three-punch) combination, which increases the probability of a finishing technique compared to a blocking technique. Of course, the technique can still be used as a block at this point, but following the internal logic of block-counter-finish, we will show the application as a striking technique here.

» The low block as a deflection technique to the opponent's thigh or abdomen has already been shown in the fifth Poomsae. Alternatively, the low block from above can go into the crook of the aggressor's elbow and control it.

» The turn after the hand edge strike to the neck (movement 12.2) provides another good opportunity for a hip throw. However, Poomsae follows up with a kick.

» Also new is the block at medium height with the hand ball "Batangson-Momtong-makgi." This movement can be used to defend against a variety of possible attacks. Here we show the defense against a kick and a takedown defense. In the latter case the technique is executed as a strike to the side of the attacker's head.

3

Fig. 139

4.1

Fig. 140

4.2

Fig. 141

Depending on the distance to the opponent, a hammer fist strike to the lower jaw or ear, in this case to the large ear nerve (auriculotemporalis) can be executed (Fig. 141).

5

Fig. 142

Moving to the "Blind Side" of the opponent

6.1

Fig. 143

Spinning kick (Dollyeo Chagi) to the solar plexus of the attacker

6.2

Fig. 144

The standard version of the technique is ideal for the powerful blocking of punches, whereby the opponent is hit on the radial nerve. Beware of follow-up techniques, the second hand is not under control yet.

6.3

Fig. 145

7.1

Fig. 146

7.2

Fig. 147

Pull and strike, control of the opponent is not given up if possible.

8.1

Fig. 148

8.2

Fig. 149

9.1

Fig. 150

The opponent's attempted chokehold is pushed aside here. The hand that executed the block then immediately grabs the opponent and pulls him close. The punch and knee strike are aimed at the liver (Fig. 148-150).

9.2

Fig. 151

The fist strike here goes to the asterion (weak point of the skull)

10

Fig. 152

11

Fig. 153

After the attempt to be grabbed has been fended off the defender grabs the wrist of the attacker and immediately executes a palm strike to the carotid artery (Fig. 152 and Fig. 153).

12.1

Fig. 154

A knee kick instead of a spin kick with a very close opponent

Turn

Fig. 155

12.2

Fig. 156

After the knee kick, the defender grabs the attacker's arm and performs the turn as in the Poomsae. The opponent is thrown over the shoulder or hip and then pinned to the ground (Fig. 155 and 156).

13.1

13.2

Fig. 157

Fig. 158

The center block strikes here with the forearm to the lower jaw

In this example, the knee strike and forearm strike are executed against a new attacker, who attempts to grab the defender by the lapels (Fig. 157 and 158).

14

Fig. 159

15.1

Fig. 160

15.2

Fig. 161

Here, the low block is used in an attempt to strip the opponent's grip. Watch out for the opponent's punching hand! After both hands are controlled, a kick and a forearm strike complete the sequence.

16

Fig. 162

Early block with the open left hand (the right hand protects).

17

Fig. 163

Same movement, but here as a knife hand strike to the neck

18.1

Fig. 164

The palm block knocks the kick attempt to the side.

Hand edge block executed once as a defensive technique and then as a strike to the neck. The attacker's hand continues to be controlled. This is followed by an attack with a straight stomping kick.

18.2

Fig. 165

19.1

Fig. 166

The palm block as a defense against a throw

19.2

Fig. 167

In Figs. 166 and 167 we see how the defender thwarts an attempted takedown. The attacker approaches with his head at stomach height. The well-timed defense is followed by a fist strike to the head.

4.3 Taegeuk Chil-Jang

1

2.1

2.2

Fig. 168

Defense against an attempted grip to the thighs . . .

Fig. 169

. . . If the opponent's head is still in a low position, a knee strike follows.

The forearm block to the inside, "Palmok-Momtong An Makgi" – here as an elbow strike. Note the second hand, which performs the "countermovement" and pulls the opponent closer for more control.

Fig. 170

The most important facts about "Poomsae 7" at a glance:

- In the seventh Poomsae, it is clear to see that the technical variety is increasing. Where in the lower Poomsae rather simple basic techniques are used, Poomsae 7 offers an alternative to the straight fist strike, at least in some places. In particular, we find more fist strikes and ball of the hand techniques. It should also be mentioned that in the seventh Poomsae, for the first time, a punch is performed with two fists at the same time (double fist). Also new: the execution of two hand techniques in succession with the same hand. Both are natural extensions of the repertoire given to us by forms 1-6. Assuming that the advanced student has already developed a better feel for the techniques, alternatives are offered here.

- The "tiger foot position" or Beom-Seogi is new. The "sinking in" on the (rear) standing leg offers a few new possibilities. These include:

  - By shifting the weight to the supporting leg, the free leg becomes "lighter" and this allows kicking techniques to be executed in a flash.

  - The shift in weight can be used to pull the opponent toward you, and thus throw them off balance.

  - The energy of letting yourself fall can be "converted" into the technique with appropriate practice, giving it a stronger effect.

- The two-handed low block in Dwit-Gubi Seogi (moves 5 and 6) can be understood and used as a throwing technique via the upper leg.

- Two hand techniques in succession with the same hand! (moves 7.1 and 7.2, 8.1 and 8.2)

3

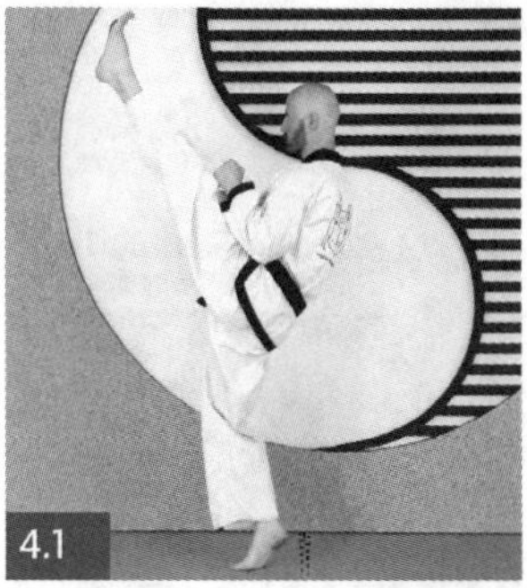
4.1

4.2

The "asterion" is the cranial fossa at the side of the back of the head where the temporal bone, parietal bone and occipital bone meet. Depending on the force applied, blows to this area can cause great damage.

Fig. 171

The opponent (perhaps a wrestler) tries to throw us . . .

Fig. 172

. . . on our back. The defense is followed by a knee strike.

Fig. 173

This is followed by a downward elbow onto the asterion.

5

Fig. 174

6

Fig. 175

Movements 5 and 6 are performed twice in succession. This can be read to mean that different types of attacks can be countered with one and the same movement pattern, in such a way that a different effect can be achieved. Fig. 174 shows the well-known "low block." Figs. 175 and 176 show the movement in close combat used as a throw.

Fig. 176

7.1

Fig. 177

Reach for the lapel, one hand controls, the other strikes.

7.2

Fig. 178

The right hand performs a second punching technique in succession.

8.1

Fig. 179

The defender reacts to a grip on the lapel by controlling the attacking hand of the opponent. It is immediately countered with a palm strike to the chin. Knockout point, see "Pain points" in the appendix.

8.2

Fig. 180

The movement of the back fist strike is described here as a lever . . .

9

Fig. 181

. . . technique shown against the shoulder. A "transportation technique."

10.1

Fig. 180 shows a second variant of the moving pattern "back fist strike." It is used as a shoulder lock. In Fig. 181 the second hand supports the lock to form an even tighter fixation (or a transportation lock).

Fig. 182

10.2

Fig. 183

The left hand blocks, and the right hand strikes back . . .

11.1

Fig. 184

. . . or both hands control the opponent's arms.

11.2

Fig. 185

Variant 3: The attacker is directly "pulled into the blow."

The scissor block or Gawi Makgi combines block and counterattack in one technique. The basic principle of the technique is to pull one of the opponent's arms downwards while counterattacking with the other hand at the same time.

12

Fig. 186

13

Fig. 187

14

Fig. 188

The wedge block (hecheo makgi) is followed by a knee strike and a double fist strike under the ribcage. Here, important organs, namely the liver and spleen, are hit simultaneously.

15

Fig. 189

The opponent is pulled forward and punched.

Rotation

Fig. 190

The rotation can be used as a lever or for evasion.

16

Fig. 191

Movement 15 (cross block) is shown here as a striking technique to the side of the head, whereby the opponent is pulled forward at the same time. The following turn can be combined with an arm lock, for example.

17

Fig. 192

18

Fig. 193

19

Fig. 194

In the repetition of the sequence, we want to understand the last movement as a finishing blow before changing the direction. We therefore assume a punch to the back of the opponent's head, while holding him back.

20

Fig. 195

21.1

Fig. 196

21.2

Fig. 197

After the back fist strike to the temple a destabilizing kick to the attackers legs follows (Pyeojeok-Chagi). A blow with the elbow to the back of the head finishes. Alternatively, a choke technique could also be applied.

22

Fig. 198

23.1

Fig. 199

23.2

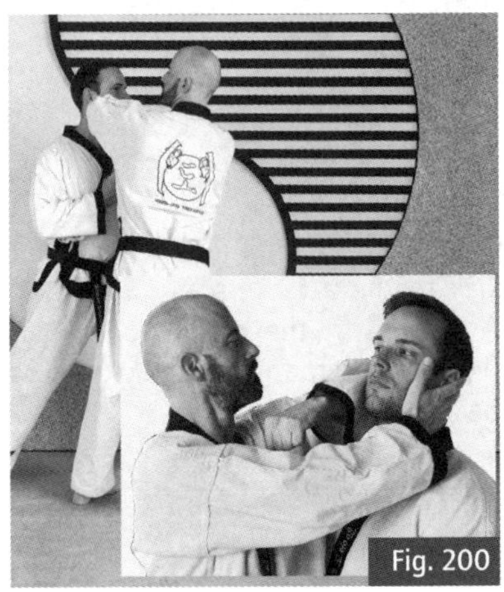
Fig. 200

The kick with the shin to the inside of the knee can be an effective weapon to break the balance of the opponent. The quickly executed elbow strike completes the action.

24

Fig. 201

25

Fig. 202

The defender remains in the forward movement until there is nothing more to expect from the attacker. Here too, as is so often the case in Poomsae, we see a determined approach against the aggressor at the end of the form.

4.4 Taegeuk Pal-Jang

1

Fig. 203

2

Fig. 204

Sprung

Fig. 205

The forearm block with the fist turned forward in close combat: One hand of the opponent is secured while the other executes a fist strike to the lower jaw!

The most important facts about "Poomsae 8" at a glance:

» The eighth Poomsae offers combinations both in static execution and in dynamic forward movement.

» Remarkable is, right at the beginning of the form, the, compared to the other forms, much more determined and dynamic beginning. After the fighting stance, which can be used as first defensive technique, there is immediately a determined counterattack in the form of a fist strike followed by a double jump kick forward (Dubaldangseong Chagi). This follow-up by two (or three) consecutive attacking movements right at the beginning of the form is new.

» The front double jump kick, the Dubaldangseong Chagi, appears in the eighth Poomsae for the first time and is used toward the end of the form in a slightly different form, namely as two separately executed kicks, Ap Chagi and Ttwieo-Ap-Chagi jump kick!

» Movements 5 and 7, the "double block," can be interpreted as a release against a grip to both arms from behind.

» Movement 18, the low block, can be understood as a throwing technique, similar to those in the seventh Poomsae, but here the pants are grabbed in the area of the thighs with both hands and the opponent is then leveraged over the thigh near the hip.

» The last eight techniques are two sequences of four, where the elbow technique is either a direct counterstrike (after the hand edge block) or a second release technique against a grip to the wrist. The back fist strike can still be part of this release or, depending on the situation, a punching technique. This sequence consists of up to three consecutive defensive techniques and a counterattack, or of a defensive movement and three consecutive counterattack techniques.

3.1

Fig. 206

3.2

Fig. 207

This position in relation to the opponent is called the blind side.

3.3

Fig. 208

After the Palmok An Makgi (Fig. 206), which strikes the elbow joint with a counter move, the defender remains on the outside (blind side). From there he delivers a counter fist strike to the liver.

3.4

Fig. 209

4

Fig. 210

5

Fig. 211

Movement no. 5 can be used as a release against an attack from behind with both hands to the wrists. Here, a turning movement must be executed as shown in the Poomsae (arrow).

6

Fig. 212

7

Fig. 213

One hand goes up and the turning of the body frees from the grip

8

Holding the opponent back by the shoulder (Poomsae step 8) can alternatively, also be performed by the neck. This variation is shown in Fig. 212.

Fig. 214

As an alternative to Fig. 212, here the hand controls the opponent's arm.

9

Fig. 215

Open block with attention on the attacker's second hand

10

Fig. 216

With this blow there is still the danger of a counterattack.

11.1

Fig. 217

With an Ap-Chagi kick the leg has the reach advantage.

The open block of movement 9 is identical to movement 1 except for the open hands. The open block is well suited to grab the opponent and draw him closer after defending against a blow.

11.2

Fig. 218

The palm block to the head thwarts the attack

12

Fig. 219

Both arms can be used here for control . . .

13.1

Fig. 220

. . . followed up with a kick to the stomach or abdomen.

The attacker tries to grab us by the hips or thighs to throw us. The palm block is used to fend off this throw and to deliver a blow to the head (Fig. 218).

Fig. 221

. . . followed by a fist thrust to the solar plexus . . .

Fig. 222

. . . the elbow lever finally fixes the attacker.

Fig. 223

The same technique (Batangson Arae Makgi) here as an elbow strike or as a control (lever) technique. If the technique is used as a lever, the ball of the hand should exert pressure at the base of the triceps (Fig. 222).

16.1

Fig. 224

16.2

Fig. 225

17

Fig. 226

18

Fig. 227

The Geodeureo Palmok Arae Makgi is shown here in the application as a throwing technique. The opponent is thrown near the center of gravity over the thigh. Very close contact with the opponent is necessary to apply the throwing technique.

Fig. 228

19.1

Jump

Fig. 229

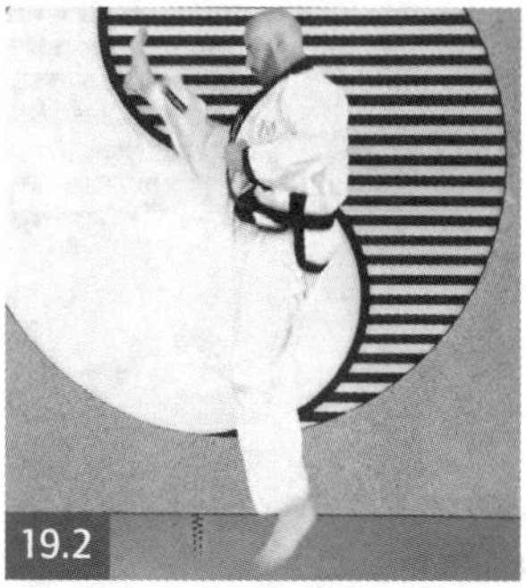

19.2

Fig. 230

19.3

Fig. 231

19.4

Fig. 232

The jump Ap-Chagi can be executed very effectively against the tip of the opponent's chin. This, however, is only recommended for experienced athletes. Alternatively, the abdomen can be used as a target area (Fig. 230).

19.5

Fig. 233

20

Fig. 234

Control of the attacking hand including a blow to the carotid artery

21

Fig. 235

One hand fixes the opponent's "gripping hand" while the second executes a strike to the neck (Fig. 234). The elbow in movement 21 serves as a release against a grip to the wrist (Fig. 235).

22

Fig. 236

23

Fig. 237

24

Fig. 238

Movement 22 can be used both as the second part of the liberation movement (in conjunction with 21) or (if you already have a "free hand") as a follow-up fist strike.

25

Fig. 239

26

Fig. 240

27

Fig. 241

Fig. 239 shows an alternative sequence. Here the elbow strike goes to the lower jaw and the "back fist strike" blocks a counterattack attempt by the attacker (Fig. 240). The fist strike then finishes.

4.5 Examples of the multifunctionality of the basic techniques

Arae Makgi (Hadan Makgi)

The low block or Arae Makgi. A simple but very effective release against a grip on the wrist. When executed correctly it hits exactly the attacker`s radial nerve. The counter move of the second hand greatly increases the effect of the release and must therefore be taken into account.

Here the defender is grabbed by the lapels. The low block is executed in the picture with the left hand against the crook of the attacker's elbow. This prevents the attacker from using his hand. At the same time he is pulled forward and destabilized by the blow to the crook of the elbow.

In some situations, the technique can also be used as a punch. This technique serves as a distraction or diversion for a subsequent technique. Delivering a strike to the abdomen can induce the opponent to neglect his guard and that can up new possibilities.

Momtong Makgi (Jungdan Makki)

The "classic" application of the forearm block to the inside. Please note that the hand that executes the block is also suitable for setting a counter. Similar to the "tying up" of a blade in fencing, where the same blade leads the attack after the parry.

If the movement is used as an arm lever against the triceps, it is best to try to push with the ulna about a hand's width above the elbow as firmly as possible against the muscle. The more the opponent is pulled (with the other hand), the better the lever works.

As a hammer fist strike against the lower jaw, the An Makgi has a devastating effect. The blow is executed as a slight whip-like movement to the side of the chin tip and can render the opponent unconscious. The rotation of the upper body and hips add power to the strike.

Ulgul Makgi (Chukyo Makki)

Here, the blocking arm is pulled upwards rapidly and interrupts the opponent's attempt to grab the shoulder or neck. The anticipating (foreshadowing) blocking of an attack is always the best option, as the opponent is not yet able to grab properly.

In this situation, the defender was already grabbed by the neck. The "high block" now knocks away an attacking hand upwards. The other hand is used to control the opponent's second hand.

The third variant can be used against the same attack as in situation 2 (grip to the neck). Now only one hand is used to control the opponent's both hands. The (free) second hand delivers a direct strike to the opponent's neck or lower jaw. Whereby the strike is conducted with the forearm.

Sonal Momtong Makgi (Sudo Taebi Makki)

Defense of a straight or hook fist punch with the open block (Geodeureo Sonal Momtong-makgi). The back hand controls here after a grip to the lapel. Both hands of the defender remain operational. Grabbing or techniques with both hands are possible.

Against a grip on the lapel the "rear" hand (i.e. the hand closer to the body) can secure the attacking hand. The (free) lead hand can strike to the opponent's neck (see appendix Pain points). This counter strike can be executed with the edge of the hand as well as with the forearm.

A variant of the option shown above is shown here. The defender presses preventively against the attacker's upper arm to stop him from striking early. The back hand is ready to defend, but could also strike or stab preventively.

Pyonsonkeut Jireugi (Kwansu Tulki)

The defender's left hand blocks and controls the attacker's lead hand by pushing it downwards. This clears the way for a thrust with the fingertips toward the opponent's eyes.

An alternative application of the technique is the hip throw. The "thrust" is used to grab behind the opponent and throw him over the hip.

Another option is to use a shoulder lever. Here, the defender's hand "stabs" between the arm and body. The second hand then strengthens the grip by grasping the defender's own hand. By turning the body the opponent can then be easily locked.

Deung Jumeok Ap-Chigi

The motion sequence of the back fist strike can be used very well as a release or leverage technique (for example, after the attacker's right hand grabs the defender's right hand). After the turn, only use the second hand to lock the lever.

Of course, the movement can be used as a blow with the back of the fist or the knuckles against the tip of the nose, the philtrum (corner of the nose), as well as on the eyebrows or the upper jaw. The technique is painful, but does not necessarily incapacitate the opponent.

If the defender is grabbed by the shoulder, the circular move can be applied as a shoulder lever, which can be used as a control or transportation technique. In the seventh Poomsae, the fixation after the shoulder lever is shown (see Fig. 181).

Gawi Makgi

The Gawi Makgi is basically a simultaneous use of the low block "Arae Makgi" with one hand and the middle block "Momtong Magki" with the other. This makes it possible to handle several attacks at different heights at the same time.

Here, the low block part of the technique is used to control the opponent's grip and the hand, the hand executing the middle block makes a striking movement with the radial side of the forearm to the lower jaw of the attacker.

Here, the low block was set earlier so that the opponent could not yet take hold. The defensive movement is combined here with a direct and simultaneous counterattack.

Appendix

1 Pain points

In the applications, the attacks are always aimed at certain points or zones that are particularly suitable for attacks, as the strongest effect can be expected at precisely these points. We want to divide the most attractive targets into two categories here, absolute knockout points, i.e. primary targets (left) and points that also cause damage but do not necessarily lead to fainting or incapacitation, the secondary targets (right).

This selection is arbitrary and is based on many years of experience. Furthermore, we do not differentiate between points as opposed to hit zones. Points where the effect is independent of a millimeter-precise hit are ideal anyway.

A: The eye offers the advantage that it is usually exposed, which means clearly visible and therefore easier to hit than other pain points. Stabs or scratches (even with low physical strength) are very painful and severely impair the opponent. Nevertheless, it should be borne in mind that an eye stab may not incapacitate the opponent. A follow-up technique should therefore be considered if a quick escape is not possible.

B: It is no coincidence that the tip of the chin, especially when hit from the side, is the primary target for boxers. Knockout punches are largely delivered at this point. One explanation is the twisting of the cervical spine along two axes, which this blow triggers. Fainting is often the result of this trauma.

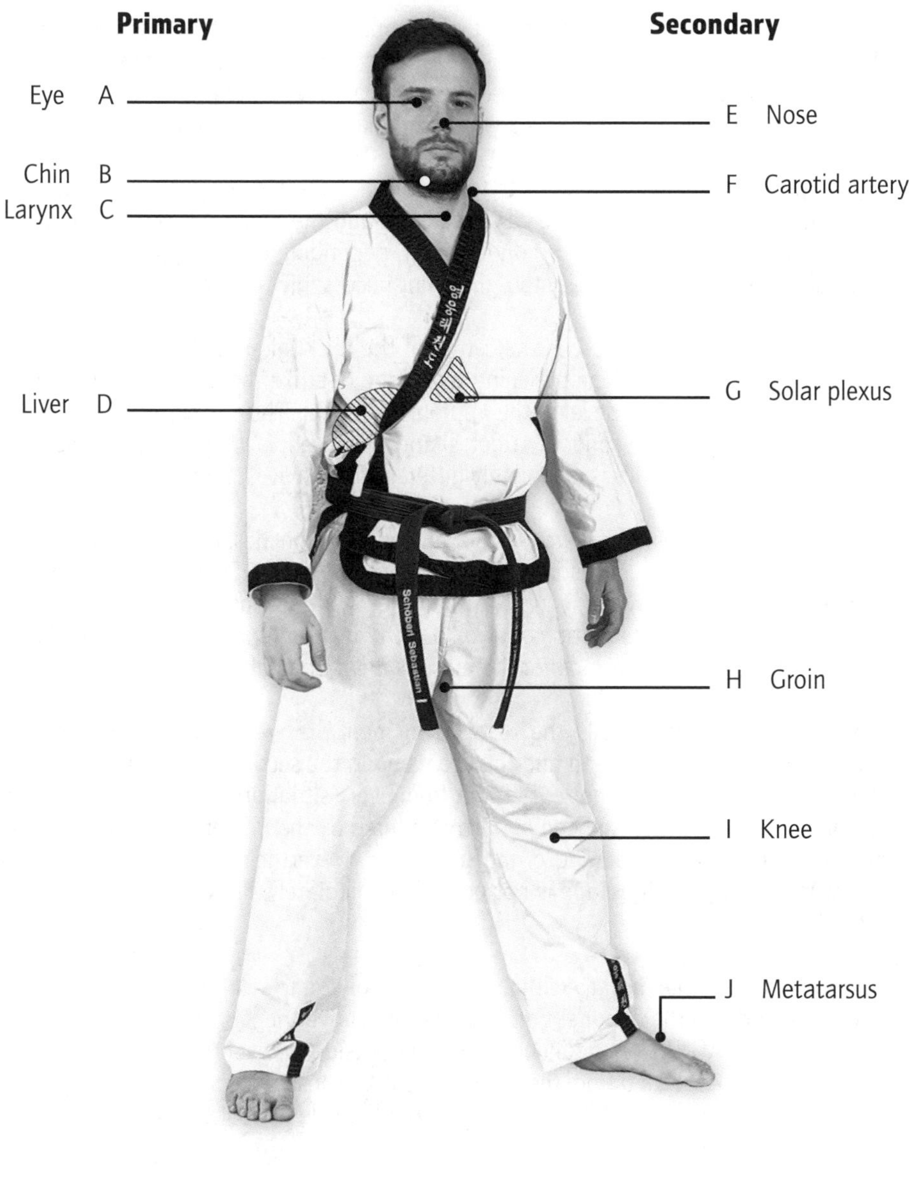

C: Blows to the larynx are very painful. They often lead to breathing problems and other complications can occur. Although this point does not trigger fainting, we list it here as a primary target due to its danger, its ease of identification and its strong effect in any case.

D: The same applies to the liver as to the tip of the chin. The liver hook is rightly feared among boxers. If the liver is hit by a punch or kick, it is almost impossible to withstand such a hit. This is basically independent of the opponent's subjective perception of pain. If the liver is hit, you can't breathe, at least for a few minutes. In unfavorable cases, a liver rupture can occur, which would have fatal consequences. Due to the size of the organ and its well-known location, the liver is a worthwhile target in an emergency.

E: In this specific case, the nose refers to the tip of the nose. Hit with a fist or the ball of the hand straight from the front. The cartilage is hit and the blow causes pain and possibly a strong flow of tears. It should be noted that, depending on the opponent's sensitivity (insensitivity) to pain, incapacity to fight is not necessarily to be expected.

F: Especially if the carotid artery in the center of the neck (glomus caroticum) is hit, it can become a knockout blow. The punching technique to strike the right place from the side requires some training to develop the appropriate effect. This is also the reason why the point is listed here as a secondary target, simply because it is not possible for everyone to effectively strike here (this is completely different for the eyes, for example).

G: The solar plexus is commonly known as a hit zone for punches. It is particularly useful if you do NOT want to cause lasting injury to your opponent. Of course, there can also be complications here. However, you will usually recover quite quickly after a brief loss of breath. In an emergency situation or if you are physically inferior, it is not advisable to use the solar plexus as a strike zone for the reasons mentioned above.

H: The abdomen, or specifically the testicles in men, are well known hit zones. It may therefore come as a surprise to find this area among the secondary targets. This is due to the following reasons: It is not easy to hit from every situation. The individual sensitivity to pain is very subjective and can be further altered by the influence of drugs. A hit does not necessarily lead to fainting or incapacitation. Nevertheless it will be a worthwhile target in many cases. If escape is not possible immediately, it may be advisable to seek a finish.

I: An attack to the knee (usually with a Yeop-Chagi or stomp kick) is in certain situations a good way to throw the opponent off balance, or deprive them of their mobility. However, attacks should ALWAYS be launched from the outside or, even better in close combat, from the inside. Attacking from the front makes little sense, especially if the other person's knee is slightly bent. So it is best to attack from the side and, of course, only in absolute emergency situations, as this can lead to nasty injuries.

J: A stomping attack on the opponent's metatarsal bone can be extremely painful and may even lead to a fracture of the metatarsal bone, which restricts mobility. This technique is usually used in conjunction with other techniques. It can be used either as a distraction or to initiate an attack in some self-defense sequences. It appears explicitly in some forms.

2 "Pedigree" of the nine founding styles of modern Taekwondo

Master (style)	Founder	Style Name (style taught)	Influences from
Funakoshi Gichin/ Funakoshi Gigo (Karate [Shotokan])	Won Kuk Lee	CHUNG DO KWAN (Tang Soo Do)	Taekkyon, Chuan Fa (Kung-Fu), Okinawa Karate, Shotokan Karate
Yang Kuk Jin (Tai Chi Chuan)	Hwan Kee	MOO DUK KWAN (Tang Soo Do)	Taekkyon, Chuan Fa (Kung-Fu), Kuk Sool, Tai-Chi-Chuan, Shotokan Karate, Okinawa Karate
Funakoshi Gichin (Karate [Shotokan])	Byung Jik Ro	SONG MOO KWAN (Tang Soo Do)	Taekkyon, Subak, Shotokan Karate
Kanken Toyama (Karate [Shudokan])	Byung In Yoon	YMCA KWON BOP BU KWAN (Kong Su Do = Tang Soo Do)	Chuan Fa (Kung-Fu), Shotokan Karate, Tai-Chi-Chuan
Unknown (Judo and Karate) Kyung Suk Lee (Judo)	Sang Sap Chun	YUN MOO KWAN (Tang Soo Do)	Judo, Karate
–	–	–	Korean War (1950-1953)

Master/former Dojang (style)	Founder	Style Name (style taught)	Influences from
Sang Sap Chun/ YUN MOO KWAN	Lee Kyo Yoon	HAN MOO KWAN (Tang Soo Do)	Judo, Karate, Tang Soo Do
Kim Hyun Soo, Funakoshi Gichin (Karate [Shotokan])/ CHUNG DO KWAN	Choi Hong Hi, Nam Tae Hi, Han Cha Kyo	OH DO KWAN (Tang Soo Do)	Taekkyon, Chuan Fa (Kung-Fu), Okinawa Karate, Shotokan Karate, Tang Soo Do
KWON BOP BU KWAN	Park Chul Hee Hong Jong Pyo	KANG DUK KWAN (Tang Soo Do)	Chuan Fa (Kung-Fu), Shotokan Karate, Tai-Chi-Chuan Tang Soo Do
CHUNG DO KWAN	Lee Wong Woo	JUNG DO KWAN	Taekkyon, Chuan Fa (Kung-Fu), Okinawa Karate, Shotokan Karate, Tang Soo Do

3 Terms

The following is a short version of the most important Korean terms and techniques. In addition to the English name, the table also shows the designation in World Taekwondo and in the styles, ITF and traditional Taekwondo.

Technique	Name WT	Name ITF / Trad. TKD
Block techniques	Makgi	Makgi
Low block	Arae-Makgi	Najune Makgi, Hadan Makgi
Mid section block	Momtong-Makgi	Kaunde Makgi, Jungdan Makgi
High block	Ulgul-Makgi	Nopunde Makgi, Sangdan Makgi
Knife hand block	Sonal-Makgi	Sonkal Makgi, Sudo Makgi
Forearm block	Palmok-Makgi	Palmok Makgi, Palmok Makgi
Stances	Seogi	Sogi
Standing, legs closed	Pyonhi-Seogi	Moa Sogi
Ready stance	Junbi-Seogi	Naranhi Sogi, Naranhi Sogi
Horse stance	Juchum-Seogi	Annun Sogi, Kima Sogi
Long walking stance	Ap-Gubi Seogi	Gunnun Sogi, Chongul Sogi
Weight back leg (L-Stance)	Dwit-Gubi Seogi	Niunja Sogi, Hugul-Seogi
Short walking stance	Ap-Seogi	Ap Sogi, Ap Sogi
Cross stance	Kkoa-Seogi	Kyocha Sogi, Kyocha Sogi
Tiger stance	Beom-Seogi	Dwitbal Sogi, Ditpal Sogi
Punch, Strike	Chigi	Taerigi, Taerigi
Kick	Chagi	Chagi
Thrust	Jireugi	Jirugi, Jirugi
Finger thrust (Knife hand thrust)	(Pyeonsonkeut-) Jireugi	(Sonkut) Tulgi, (Kwansu-)Tulki
Parts of the body		
Fist	Jumok	Joomuk (Jumok), Chongkwon
Knife hand	Sonal	Sonkal, Sudo
Back fist	Deung-Jumeok	Dung Joomuk, Dung Jumok
Hammer fist	Me-Jumeok	Me-Jumok, Me-Jumok
Elbow	Palkeup	Palkup, Palkup
Knee	Mureup	Moorup, Murup
Throat	Meok	Mok, Mok
Kicking techniques	Chagi	Chagi
Front kick	Ap-Chagi	Ap Chagi
Side kick	Yeop-Chagi	Yop Chagi
Roundhouse kick	Dollyeo-Chagi	Dollyo Chagi

Technique	Name WT	Name ITF / Trad. TKD
Axe kick	Naeryeo-Chagi	Naeryo Chagi
Pushing kick (straight)	Miro-Chagi	Miro Chagi
Back kick	Dwit-Chagi	Dwit Chagi
Back spinning kick	Momdolyo-Chagi	Bandae Dollyo, Chagi
Jumping kick	Twio-Chagi	Twimyo Chagi, Tymen Chagi
Outwards twisted kick	Biteureo-Chagi	Bituro Chagi
Directions		
Front, forward	Ap	Ap
Inside, to the inside	An	An/Anuro
Outside, to the outside	Bakkat	Bakkat/Bakuro
Downwards	Naeryeo	Naeryo
Upwards	Ollyeo	Ollyo, e.g., Chukyo
Left	Oen	Wen
Right	Oreun	Orun

4 Spelling

The translation of Korean terms and sounds into German/English is a notoriously tricky matter, which neither the McCune-Reischauer transcription (from 1984) nor by the revised Korean romanization (since2000) (cf. *https://de.wikipedia.org/wiki/Revidierte_Romanisierung*), solved completely, which perhaps never will be completely possible. The omission of breve and apostrophes in the revised romanization is basically a positive development. The usage of double vowels for Korean sounds to transfer to English seems to be a fair enough approximation. In any case, the present work attempts to stay with the WT writing. Some of the ITF or traditional writings are so to say "freestyle" and often were written just as people thought them to be sounding approximately correct. In the table with the terms, the current spelling (WT) is used in the (middle) column. In the right-hand column the older spellings from sources before the second Romanization are used in some cases. This is to show that one and the same technique is described.

With the new spelling, it should be noted that "ae" and "eu" are single, almost voiceless vowels "ah"' and "oo." The letter "w"' in "Dwit-Chagi," for example, is de facto not audible. As this book is intended as a practical exercise book and provides insights into the applicability of Taekwondo as a realistic self-defense System, the original sound of the words is not our focus. Still we are as accurate as possible. All techniques are described in English and therefore it should be easy to understand how they work in most of the cases. The use of Korean terms is primarily for the benefit of the active Taekwondoins to be able to identify the respective technique from the training.

5 About the author

Sandro Stückler began his Taekwondo career on March 10, 1993. For the first few years he trained with the Korean grandmasters Yoon Dong Il (8th Dan) and Park Seung Kwan (8th Dan). After the dojang moved, he focused for a few years on the throwing and lever techniques of Hap Ki Do under Master Gilbert Neuwirth (5th Dan). He then spent some time with Grandmaster Shin Ik-Jin (8th Dan). After completing his studies in architecture, he trained in traditional Taekwondo (the System of Master Kwon Jae Hwa using Hyung forms) under KwanJangnim Master Dr. Andreas Held (6th Dan). For 10 years now, "Kyosanim" Sandro Stückler has been in charge of the schools in Graz, which belong to the largest Austrian system for traditional Taekwondo 'YU-TAEKWONDO'.

He trains people of every age in the Korean martial art. Courses for Taekwondo and virtues at schools and self-protection courses at public institutions are frequently held. He also runs camps with great enthusiasm, where the focus is on intensively training the many interested students and providing them with lots of practical exercises as in-depth knowledge as well. Topics such as meditation and philosophy round off his area of interest and workshops and seminars on these topics can be attended several times a year.

A flying Yeop-Chagi, shown by the author at a training workshop in Graz

6 Bibliography

Taekwondo Textbook Kukkiwon, Osung Publishing Company 2005

ODO KWAN TANG SOO DO KOREA'S KARATE – Creation, History and Evolution Losik Len 2016

FROM CREATION TO UNIFICATION – The Complete History Behind the Ch'ang Hon (ITF) Patterns, Anslow Stuart 2013

ZEN-KUNST DER SELBSTVERTEIDIGUNG TAEKWON-DO-KARATE, Kwon Jae-Hwa 1971/1976

YIN UND YANG – Das kosmische Grundmuster in den Kulturformen Chinas, Fiedeler Frank 1993

I CHING DAS BUCH DER WANDLUNGEN, Wilhelm Richard 1972

Erfahrungen mit dem I GING – Vom kreativen Umgang mit dem Buch der Wandlungen, Diederichs Ulf 1984

Sinn des I Ging, Wilhelm Hellmut 1972 LAOTSE – Tao Te King, Wilhelm Richard 1957

LIÄ DSI – Quellender Urgrund, Wilhelm Richard 1972

TAEKWONDO – Koreanischer Kampfsport, Gil Konstantin 1990

TAEKWONDO PERFEKT 1 – Die Formenschule bis zum Blaugurt, Gil Konstantin, Kim ChulHwan 1999

TAEKWONDO PERFEKT 2 – Die Formenschule vom Blau- bis zum Schwarzgurt, Gil Konstantin, Kim Chul-Hwan 1988

KYUSHO – Angriffspunkte in Selbstverteidigung und Kampfsport, Reinisch, Höller, Maluschka 2009

DIM MAK TÖDLICHE NERVENPUNKTE, Fruth Christian 2009

7 Credits

Cover design: Anja Elsen

Interior layout: Anja Elsen

Cover photo: © Sandro Stückler

Cover illustration: © AdobeStock

Interior photos: © Sandro Stückler

Interior illustrations: © Sandro Stückler

Copy editing: Sarah Tomblin, www.sarahtomblinediting.com

Managing editor: Elizabeth Evans

Model: Sebastian Schöberl; many thanks for his patient and professional work.

Thanks to my son Alexander, who is responsible for pressing the shutter button perfectly.

THE SPORTS PUBLISHER

$24.95 US

ISBN 978-1-78255-280-2

Paul Eaglestone

FREE SPEED

A WINNING FORMULA FOR SWIM EFFICIENCY AND FASTER TRIATHLONS

Free Speed is coach Paul Eaglestone's breakthrough training method that combines efficient swimming technique with a pace-setting formula to achieve faster triathlons. In addition to explaining his own training methods, Paul also gives the triathlete the tools to design their own training sessions based on individual goals and targets, always with an eye on getting the most out of each session.

$26.95 US

978-1-78255-276-5

Sara Lyn Chana

ESSENTIAL YOGA WITH PROPS

ENHANCE EVERY POSE FOR FULL-BODY MOBILITY AND FLEXIBILITY

This is the perfect guide for yoga practitioners at all levels. Beginners are given basic instructions on correct yoga postures, whereas the use of yoga props challenges experienced yogis by improving their form and attaining precise body alignment. Those with physical disabilities and who may struggle with their own mobility and balance are encouraged to practice yoga with the support of props. Using props makes yoga accessible to everyone.

MEYER & MEYER Sport
Von-Coels-Str. 390
52080 Aachen
Germany

Phone +49 02 41 - 9 58 10 - 13
Fax +49 02 41 - 9 58 10 - 10
E-Mail sales@m-m-sports.com
Website www.m-m-sports.com

MEYER & MEYER SPORT